LOST GRAND HOTELS *of* CLEVELAND

MICHAEL DEALOIA

THE History PRESS

Published by The History Press
Charleston, SC 29403
www.historypress.net

Front cover, top center: Futuristic print of the Cleveland Hotel. *Courtesy of the Western Reserve Historical Society.*

First published 2014

Manufactured in the United States

ISBN 978.1.62619.632.2

Library of Congress CIP data applied for.

Notice: The information in this book is true and complete to the best of our knowledge. It is offered without guarantee on the part of the author or The History Press. The author and The History Press disclaim all liability in connection with the use of this book.

Much love to Nora and our wee one, Ileana. You both inspire me so!

CONTENTS

FOREWORD

The hotels most of us know best are those outside our hometowns. We stay in them while on business or holiday. Most people never get to sleep out in their own city, and if given the chance, it is likely that they will end up in a copycat cubicle similar to those experienced while on the road and find themselves dining in a branch of a chain restaurant enhanced by ersatz period décor. What we long for is a stay in the Ritz, the Waldorf or the Palace in San Francisco: a place with character, history and personality that was a product of evolution rather than managerial intelligent design. But usually, our imaginations locate that "place" outside our hometowns.

The pages that follow are about the hotels we would all love to experience—institutions with unique personalities that accreted over the years. They are places linked to some of the great personalities in American history and to some of the most interesting and quirky events in our nation's saga. They hosted presidents, epitomized the best in cuisine, provided entertainment of the highest caliber and were the settings for some of the most interesting, evil and comical foibles of humanity. Most importantly, they were all part of the history of Greater Cleveland.

Michael C. DeAloia's *Lost Grand Hotels of Cleveland* is a reminder that people once came to know Cleveland by its hotels. It was in those hotels that they formed their opinions of a community—one that was a maker of presidents during the time of the Hollenden and an industrial power in the years when the Statler and Hotel Cleveland were in their prime. These were hostelries with tradition and style, places to be seen and places to look forward to visiting. One can choose to read *Lost Grand Hotels of Cleveland* as another "what was" book about Cleveland. It is that. But it is also an important essay about an aspect of our community's history that has not been given detailed attention. More importantly, it is a reminder that a community's "brand" and image grow organically over time from many pieces and parts. For many years, a visitor's home away from home in Cleveland was a key component of the image he or she built of the city. Conversely, Clevelanders came to sense who they were when they heard about the guests who stayed at the city's great hotels or enjoyed the food and entertainment offered in their dining rooms and ballrooms. The Statler, Cleveland, Alcazar, Winton, Hollenden and other great hostelries of Cleveland may not have been the Ritz or the Waldorf, but they were among the best image makers the city has ever had.

Professor John J. Grabowski's interests and research span the fields of public and academic history. He specializes in the areas of immigration and ethnicity, local (Cleveland) urban history and public history, particularly the fields of archives and museums. He holds a joint appointment with the Department of History at Case Western Reserve University (CWRU) and the Western Reserve Historical Society as the Krieger-Mueller Associate Professor in Applied History, where he serves as historian and senior vice-president for research and publications. In addition to teaching at the department, he also oversees the World Wide Web edition of the Encyclopedia of Cleveland History/Dictionary of Cleveland Biography, a joint project of CWRU and the Western Reserve Historical Society.

PREFACE

As I wrote this preface, I was a bit comforted to know that Cleveland is currently going through a hotel renaissance. This isn't the first time hotels have become the hot commodity of development in Cleveland, and I surmise it is not the last. This book details the grand hotels of Cleveland's past—monumental and historical structures built between 1880 and 1930. Recently, Cleveland has experienced one welcomed hotel development after another, along with other exciting developments, such as the Horseshoe Casino, the Global Center on Health Innovation, the Cleveland Aquarium and an unexpected movement of millennials and empty nesters renting a large number of apartments in the downtown area. Key hotel developments announced during the last few years include:

The Flats East Bank project, which features a new 150-room Aloft Hotel, completed in June 2013.

The former Crowne Plaza Cleveland Downtown is undergoing a $70 million renovation and conversion to the Westin Cleveland Convention Center. The luxury hotel will feature LEED-certified green construction across 484 rooms, including 40 suites. The hotel's conversion is expected to be complete in April 2014.

CRM Companies recently announced its resumption of work in collaboration with Kimpton Hotels & Restaurants on the historic Schofield Building. The renovations will turn the property into a 122-room boutique hotel and fifty-five luxury residences. Construction is expected to be complete by late 2014.

Drury Hotels recently emerged as the winning bidder for the highly sought-after Cleveland Board of Education building; the company is planning to redevelop the building into a 180-room Drury Plaza Hotel.

Cleveland's apartment market reported a remarkable occupancy rate of over 96 percent as of the end of 2012. The K&D Group, Inc., purchased the Embassy Suites Cleveland Downtown in late 2012 and has begun a $3 million renovation to transform the hotel's 252 suites into 232 apartments. The removal of the Embassy Suites' inventory of hotel rooms should aid the absorption of new supply in the short term.

Cuyahoga County expects to build a new, $272 million, six-hundred-room Hilton Hotel next to the city's new convention center.

Starwood and an investor group were discussing a Le Meridien Hotel flag for the John Hartness Brown Building, a historic property between East Ninth and East Twelfth Streets. The downtown Cleveland hotel will house 206 rooms, a restaurant and bar, an indoor pool and meeting spaces.

If all of these planned hotels actually come to fruition, the present would, indeed, rival the time period focused on in this book. This wanderlust for hotels occurred roughly fifty years ago in Cleveland (which suggests that this new focus on building hotels in Cleveland is past due in occurring). The city experienced a second renaissance in the 1960s as Mayor Celebrezze, and the mayors who followed him, invested heavily in downtown renewal. Yet it was around this time that the major hotels in Cleveland—especially the Allerton, Winton, Hollenden and Statler—were either redeveloped into office buildings, low-income apartments or, in the case of Hollenden, torn down.

Celebrezze kicked off the 1960s "hotel madness" by offering the radical proposal of creating a new twenty-story Hilton Hotel on a piece of city-owned land on the edge of the downtown mall. The mall, a central park area in downtown Cleveland, had been open space since Mayor Johnson dreamed it up in the early 1900s. No one in fifty years had suggested putting any kind of commercial building on it.[1] And the mood in Cleveland then certainly did not cater to such development. The hotel development was left to die on the vine. That is not to say that in the late 1950s or early 1960s, Cleveland did not need a new hotel. It did. Cleveland desperately needed a big new downtown hotel. No really big hotel had been built since the 1920s, and the only smaller hotels, such as the Auditorium Hotel (also the Allerton Hotel), had been put up in 1926–28. By the 1960s, the old Hollenden was a firetrap, ripe for demolition. The Statler, Winton and

Hotel Cleveland, though refurbished, were inadequate. No big operator had seemed eager to fulfill the need until Hilton management suddenly offered this proposal for a skyscraper. The only spot Hilton would consider was on the piece of city-owned mall. It would be practically next door to Public Hall, where big conventions were usually held. Architecturally, the plan was attractive, but it would obviously need to rise above the five-story limitations on mall buildings.[2] Cleveland has never really been an easy place for real estate development, much less hotel development. The truth is, very few hotels have ever been a big success in Cleveland. It is as if they suffer from the "curse" of the Stillman Hotel.

THE CURSE OF THE STILLMAN HOTEL

In the early 1880s, as Cleveland was beginning to flex its industrial muscle, a trio of hopeful hotel magnates conceived of an idea of building the "finest hotel west of New York." The entrepreneurs involved included Howard Eells, Colonel W.H. Harris and Stillman Witts, and each desired a well-designed hotel that would be the talk of the town. They succeeded in building a grand structure, the likes of which had never been seen before in Cleveland, just east of the Lennox Building. The vast Lennox Building was located on the northeastern corner of Euclid Avenue and East Ninth Street, where the mostly empty Huntington Building resides today.

The front lawn of the Stillman Hotel was grand, green and beautiful. Flowers bloomed and blossomed to form a picture-perfect portrait of color. There were nightly dinners on the tiered and spacious front porches. There were grand fountains. The hotel's suites and single rooms were finely decorated. Its parlors were large and comforting. Unfortunately, not three months after opening, a great fire came along and burned up everything within its massive stone and iron walls. And while the outside of the hotel barely spoke of the fire disaster, the inside of the hotel was a hopeless wreck.

After reopening, a new general manager—Henry F. Roesser—took control of the Stillman. While managing the staff one morning, he suddenly died. His successor— a Mr. Aiken—took his own life in a fit of despondency. For a short period of time, the Stillman closed. It reopened with new management, but similar results of bad luck and no hotel guests persisted. Despite having a strong roster of "permanent guests"—including Mr. George Worthington,

Mr. Stewart Chisholm and Mr. Andrew Squire—the hotel never had much of a chance for success. Many considered the hotel too "uptown" from the train lines or Public Square. The lesson learned from the Stillman Hotel still holds true today because in real estate, the one thing more important than anything else is location, location and location.

The Golden Age Hotels of Cleveland

The old—and, I as call them, the "Golden Age"—hotels of Cleveland yore were amazing buildings. They were true living spaces, full of rich stories, some illuminating, some macabre and most pretty exciting. There were, of course, dozens of other famous Cleveland hotels, such as the American House, Hotel Westlake, the New Amsterdam Hotel, the Sterling Hotel, the Gillsy Hotel, the Tudor Arms, the Bolton Hotel, the Belmont Hotel, the Colonial Hotel, the Commodore Hotel, the Euclid Hotel, the Mecca Hotel, the Olmsted Hotel, Park Villa Place and the Wade Park Manor. But I believe the seven selected for this particular volume capture the identity of Cleveland the best.

And during this "Golden Age of Cleveland Hotels," the hotel industry was surprisingly robust and nationally influential. The hotel industry was so prominent in Cleveland that it gave rise to a number of innovative and creative entrepreneurs who created a publishing industry catering to the demands and needs of the local and national hospitality trade. A trade publication called *Hotel Life* was published and distributed by T. Melville Lewis. His offices were located near 265 Woodland Avenue. The magazine enjoyed a national following of hoteliers and vendors keen on supplying this growing industry.

The owners of the grand hotels of Cleveland formed the Cleveland Hotels' Association and began to publish their own magazine—*Around the Circle*—and it was considered a minor miracle in the hospitality industry that competitors bandied together to capture more guests. Cleveland's finest hotels participated, including those in this book, as well as the Auditorium Hotel (East Sixth Street and St. Clair), the Bolton Hotel (East Eighty-ninth and Carnegie Avenue), the Devon Hotel (located at 1588 Ansel Avenue near Wade Park and geared to the female traveler), the New Amsterdam (Euclid Avenue and East Twenty-second Street) and many other magnificent hotels. The magazine also changed with the perspective of the hotel audience from its historical permanent guest to the transient guest as it was stocked in hotel rooms every couple of weeks in the hopes that guests would take the magazine with them upon checkout.

The hospitality industry was such a big business in Cleveland that it also gave rise to the creation of the Hotel Life Tourist Bureau, located in the Williamson Building on Public Square. The bureau was the Hotels.com of its day as it dispensed information on hotels for every city in America and most major cities in Europe.

Researching the old hotels included in this book was a thrill but also a telling warning that the fortunes of a city—as they wax and wane—can be seen in the health of its hotels before it is witnessed in the well-being of the general building population. Cleveland has seen the rise and fall of its great hotels just as the city has seen its wealth, business and political influence do the same. Yet the Cleveland hotels included in this book, in my opinion, have created or crafted a rich mythos about the city's fortunes.

I am very interested to witness the fates of the new hotels in Cleveland. And I am quite thrilled to delve into the dynamic stories of Cleveland's grand hotels. I hope you enjoy them, too. We are witness to the next chapter in Cleveland's hotels, but it always wise to understand the past. And Cleveland's past with hotels is nothing short of complicated yet glorious.

ACKNOWLEDGEMENTS

Cleveland is blessed to have many wonderful historical archives. The rich history of Cleveland is well protected and preserved. It now needs to be unlocked and enjoyed. This volume of *Lost Grand Hotels of Cleveland* owes its production and research depth to several individuals. I would love to thank John Grabowski of the Western Reserve Historical Society for his magnificent foreword and his great guidance in research. One of my greatest benefactors is Bill Barrow of the *Cleveland Press* Archives. Bill took me under his wing when I was writing a very raw blog called the "Cool History of Cleveland." He has been a wonderful mentor ever since. Other key individuals in the research of this book include Ann Sindelar, archivist, and Jane Mason, vice-president of marketing, of the Western Reserve Historical Society; Greg Palumbo, director, and Amanda Francazio, archivist, at the Lakewood Historical Society; Lynn Duchez Bycko, archivist, at the *Cleveland Press* Archives; and Maureen Mullin, librarian, and Patrice Hamiter, photo archivist, at the Cleveland Public Library. A big thanks goes to John Vacha—a great local historian—who offered some needed help with research on the Hotel Hollenden.

Any book I write would not be complete without John Heaney writing the back cover copy. John and I wrote a book on the history of a small college as well, and it is always an honor to work together. Of course, my legal counsel and beautiful fiancée, Nora Loftus, deserves kudos for helping me with editing. She would also listen to my newest revelation about the book and, at times, would have to hear me complain about the rigors of writing.

But through it all, she was a pillar of strength and inspiration. Big thanks go to my dear friends Tim Coughlin, David Moss, John McCartney and Pat Walker for supporting me through the dark days of authorship. I also have to give kudos to Josh Walsh and the entire crew of Designing Interactive for allowing me to invade their workspace to finish off the book. And thank you to my family for all their support and love.

I would encourage you to join or at least visit these wonderful archives. I have no doubt they would love to see you and would offer not only great hospitality but also a wonderful story or two on Cleveland. This city has one of the best histories on the planet, and it should be investigated and relished thoroughly.

KEY LINKS

Cleveland Press Archives: http://www.clevelandmemory.org/press.
Cleveland Public Library: www.cpl.org.
Lakewood Historical Society: http://www.lakewoodhistory.org.
Western Reserve Historical Society: http://www.wrhs.org.

ALCAZAR HOTEL

The Alcazar Hotel is nestled comfortably on the leafy green corner of Surrey and Derbyshire Roads in Cleveland Heights, Ohio. Its back is turned away from the hustle and bustle of Cedar Road. The hotel rests effortlessly in an energetic neighborhood. Similar to the Lake Shore Hotel in Lakewood, Ohio, the Alcazar was once built as a refuge for the rich and famous but now serves as a residence hotel for seniors. The hotel was built with a touch of Spanish flavor and was formally dedicated on October 1, 1923. The decorative vestibule of colorful limestone featured imported Spanish tiles, duplicates of those in the Alcazar of Seville, Spain. The Alcazar of Seville was originally a Moorish fort and is now a palace for the Spanish royals. It is the oldest royal palace still in use in Europe. The Alcazar of Seville is one of the finest examples of Mudejar architecture—a type of Iberian architecture and decoration used particularly in Aragon and Castile, Spain—in the world. And the inspiration is alive and thriving at the Alcazar Hotel today.

The distinctive, five-story apartment-hotel was constructed by George W. Hale, Edna Florence Steffans, Harry E. Steffans and Kent Hale Smith.[3] The original cost of construction of the Alcazar was $1.9 million. The hotel opened with 195 rooms and a one-hundred-car-capacity underground garage. It took two years to build. The Alcazar was an apartment-hotel, which was an in-vogue living arrangement back in the 1920s. The word *alcazar* means "home in a fortress." The original owners were intimately involved with the design of the hotel. Edna Florence Steffans selected every piece of furniture for the hotel while George Hale traveled extensively to Spain to pick each of the fourteen tile patterns used in the lobby.[4] Real estate and commerce were in the blood of the developers. The Steffanses were the developers of the Cedar-Fairmount building in Cleveland Heights. Kent Hale Smith was a partner in the Everett Company, the company that actually built the Alcazar. He would go on to further fame as one of the founders of the Lubrizol Corporation.[5]

The Alcazar castle, as well as the Hotel Ponce de Leon and Cordova Hotels in St. Augustine, Florida, inspired the architect of the hotel—H.T. Jeffrey. (The Hotel Ponce de Leon was built by Henry Flagler, a partner of John D. Rockefeller in the Standard Oil Company, which was based in Cleveland, Ohio, at the time.) Jeffrey also had the honor of designing the Van Sweringen brothers' home in Shaker Heights. The Alcazar was, and still remains, a glorious, rich architectural gem. Ann E. Donken best described its design in an issue of *View from the Overlook*:[6]

> *Its long buff-colored brick façades are broken up with small iron balconies, contrasting brick quoins and terracotta friezes. The deep eaves are capped with overhanging red roof tiles. The sides of the building's irregular pentagon surround a large central courtyard with a terracotta fountain. Featuring a menagerie of spouting frogs and turtles, the fountain's design and construction were executed by the well-known firm of Fischer and Jirouch. The hotel's main lobby is outfitted in walnut and Spanish tile. It is surrounded by a loggia with arched colonnades. All of these elements combine to provide a feeling of sophistication and elegance.*

The hotel was opulence personified and hidden directly off a major avenue. It was brilliant in design, location and construction. The hotel was an oasis just a short trolley or carriage ride outside the sixth-largest city in the United States. It offered the sleepy enclave of Cleveland Heights a bit of Hollywood flair. When the Alcazar opened in 1923, it was the lead story in the *Cleveland Town Topics*, a high-society newsletter, proclaiming:

> *Picture yourself living in a castle of sun-blessed Spain…dreams of architectural perfection have come true; the tiles used in the floors and walls imported directly from Spain. The beautiful fireplace and the wonderful stairs are exact duplicates of those in the famous Casa del Greco in Old Spain.*[7]

Six short years after its dedication, in 1929, the hotel went into receivership, a victim of the Great Depression. The Union Mortgage Company took control of the hotel's stock and gave public notice of the hotel's receivership status. The hotel was eventually sold to Alcazar Inc., which was controlled by Susan Rebhan and Robb Bartholomew, for the sum of $854,200. Rebhan was best known as the campaign manager of Ohio Supreme Court judge Florence E. Allen. Allen was the first female Supreme Court justice in Ohio and, later in her career, was the first federal judge in the United States. Bartholomew was a local attorney and real estate investor.

As with most of the hotels in Cleveland, the Alcazar Hotel offered a great restaurant to its patrons and to the public. During the Depression, the Alcazar's restaurant was called the Patio Dining Room, and the cocktail lounge was the "Intimate Bar." Both would become the refined home to many stars, mobsters, athletes and journalists. By the 1960s, the hotel had a restaurant more in tune with its residence clientele as opposed to individuals seeking a culinary feast like in the old days. The restaurant was all-white tablecloth service. The focus on the restaurant was (unfortunately) the large arching windows that overlooked the hotel's courtyard and famed fountain—not the food on the menu. By the early 1980s, the restaurant was competing with a "fresh new restaurant row" on Lee Road, including the Tavern Company, which had just opened. The menu was stale, and the hotel decided to end the full kitchen service for the patrons.

By the late 1950s, the Alcazar was experiencing what other permanent guest hotels were quick to notice. Homeownership was rising. People were moving to the suburbs (even from the inner suburbs like Cleveland Heights) in droves. The hotel fell into disrepair. In 1963, Western Reserve Residences, a Christian Scientist organization, purchased the hotel for use as retirement home for members of its faith. It was soon opened up to all faiths to improve occupancy.

In mid-1960, the Alcazar went through a $250,000 remodeling of 72 of its apartments, and an additional $300,000 was targeted for the other 104 suites at the time. The hope was to maintain its current permanent resident base while attracting a new executive class that was traveling often or for long periods of time to Cleveland. The Alcazar Hotel, along with the Westlake Hotel in Rocky River, requested redevelopment grants from the federal government. The $3.4 million grant from the Department of Housing and Urban Development was set aside to rehabilitate old buildings into apartments for the elderly. The Alcazar Hotel was placed on the National Register of Historic Places in 1979.

The Comings and Goings at the Alcazar Hotel

The Alcazar Hotel, it seems, was always a center of entertainment and a refuge for entertainers. Bob Hope for many years kept a residence at the hotel. Musicians Cole Porter (who penned his "Night and Day" at the Alcazar) and George Gershwin found inspiration and relaxation at the Spanish-inspired hotel. Johnny Weissmuller and his exotic lover, Lupe Vélez, held residence there during the Great Lakes Exposition. Famed Broadway star Mary Martin (mother of actor Larry Hagman) found the Alcazar Hotel the perfect venue to enjoy some downtime during her theater runs in Cleveland. And, of course, Jack Benny was known to tell a few jokes and tall tales at the Alcazar's bar. It was quite the roster of famous folks. The Alcazar Hotel was known for its quiet surroundings and world-class service that comforted many famous and hardworking celebrities.

During 1932, the Alcazar was rocked by three robberies, all deviously perpetrated by the same shabbily dressed man. After stealing the great sum of $250 in August 1932, the robber decided that the hotel was worthy of his return business. He had a penchant for robbing the hotel at night while the same night clerk was performing her duties. Inside job? Perhaps. But more likely, the robber thought the Alcazar was a tempting and poorly guarded cash register.

The musical family the Paderewskis (singer and mom, Kay; father, George, at the piano; and son Jan at the organ) returned to Cleveland during the summer of 1954 to play at Charlie Reinholt's Intimate Bar at the Alcazar. Originally from Cleveland, the Paderewskis had a dinner club on Harvard Avenue before opening a "plush supper club" in Fort Lauderdale, Florida. From all sources, it was a noted and richly heralded return for the family musical group.

Lew Wasserman, the Hollywood mogul who built MCA Studios, grew up amid the speakeasies and silent movie palaces of Cleveland, Ohio. After graduating high school in 1930, Wasserman worked for the Mayfield Road Gang of Cleveland operating an illegal casino. He then moved to Chicago in 1936 to become a talent agent at the Music Corporation of America. Wasserman, when coming back to Cleveland to promote his ever-growing list of top talent, would ply local journalists and theater critics with booze, broads and food at the Alcazar Hotel. Famed *Plain Dealer* drama critic William F. McDermott was a constant fixture in the bar and ballroom as well.

For a period of time, the Alcazar Hotel had a supper club that adjoined the hotel's dining room. It could accommodate 125 dancers. Opening night was reserved for only high-society blue-bookers who received an engraved invitation for the special evening. Beth Parks, a famous Scottish singer, was a headline at the supper club during its heyday. She would sing show tunes from *Brigadoon*, *Finian's Rainbow* and *Gentlemen Prefer Blondes*. Pianists Howie Mather and Vince Parish also experienced a good run at the Alcazar's supper club. Mather was a veteran of the supper club scene, and Parish played piano at the Commodore Hotel and the Cleveland Athletic Club.

In 1958, there were a series of ads run in the local newspapers offering an open house to meet Mrs. Frances Schuerman—"the most talked about housewife in Ohio today." She had appeared in a *Saturday Evening Post* article earlier that year that detailed her battle with her weight and her success in losing weight on the Staffer Home Plan. The local Staffer office was, for a time, based out of the Alcazar Hotel. It is a fascinating first look into the modern multibillion-dollar weight loss business.

The Alcazar Fencing Club

Bill Reith had a mission. As a world-class fencer, he dreamed he could bring his passion to underprivileged youth in Cleveland. Reith was, perhaps, the finest athlete to graduate from Fenn College (now Cleveland State University). During his junior year at Fenn, Reith won the All-Ohio epee title and was fourth in the Midwest Championships. As a senior, he had a season record of 41-7. He was on the U.S. World Championship teams of 1974, 1975 and 1977 and won a gold medal at the USA Pan American Games in 1975. He started the Alcazar Fencing Club in 1977, when he found he could use one of the old ballrooms as a practice facility. Many of the participants were African American youth who might never have had access to the Olympic sport if it weren't for Reith and the old hotel that desperately needed an infusion of energy. Many of his pupils went on to compete at the Junior Olympic championships. At one point, he had nearly sixty active students at his Alcazar Fencing Club. And after the noise of the saber rattling literally got too loud, Reith and his famous fencing club were asked to leave the once grand hotel. But for a number of years, the Alcazar was producing a long list of world-class and nationally competitive fencers.

THE ALCAZAR TODAY

The Alcazar Hotel has served as a senior citizen independent-living residence for over forty years. By 2004, the hotel function of the Alcazar was finally closed. However, the hotel does offer a limited bed-and-breakfast experience, as well as some modest corporate housing. Occasionally, the hotel will host weddings and small parties. But the events fail to compare to the raucous, Hollywood star–studded parties that the Alcazar used to host. The Alcazar was, and remains, one of Cleveland's grandest residential hotels and was among the first in the suburbs. While originally appealing to wealthy Clevelanders, it appeals now to clientele looking to live in a fashionable, architecturally stunning palace on a budget. There is nothing like it in the Cleveland area with its Spanish inspiration and its fabled history. The Alcazar rests quietly in a residential neighborhood not calling too much attention to itself. Keeping its robust and fun past silent is, of course, a challenge. Of all the hotels in this book, the Alcazar remains unique and iconic. Its residents whisper the frolicking stories of its amazing past. The doors to the hotel open to all who wander in, curious about what other secrets the hotel keeps.

Left: The famous Alcazar Fencing Team practices for its next competition. *Photo courtesy of the* Cleveland Press *Archives.*

Opposite: The dazzling entrance of the Alcazar Hotel. *Photo courtesy of the* Cleveland Press *Archives.*

RESTAURANT

A courtesy vehicle was ready to take patrons of the Alcazar to their favorite haunts. *Photo courtesy of the* Cleveland Press *Archives.*

Welcome to the grand Alcazar Hotel. *Photo courtesy of the Cleveland Public Library.*

ALLERTON HOTEL

The *Plain Dealer*'s real estate editor—J.G. Monnet—proudly announced the birth of the Allerton Hotel in a May 13, 1923 column. The Allerton Hotel chain, with regal properties in New York and Chicago, announced a new "bachelor hotel" to be constructed on the southwest corner of East Thirteenth Street and Chester Avenue. (The Chicago Allerton still exists and is widely considered one of the nation's grand hotels.) Crowell & Little received the contract to build the sixteen-story stone, brick and steel structure. Murgatroyd & Ogden was the architect of this beautifully designed hotel, as it was on all of the Allerton properties. The tower is actually the equivalent of twenty stories high, as the extra space above the room floors were used for elevators, heating and other mechanicals.

Called "Cleveland's friendly skyscraper," the Hotel Allerton was opened for inspection on November 10, 1926. Consistent with the other hotels in the famous Allerton chain, the new hotel featured extensive sports rooms, including a swimming pool and squash, handball and tennis courts. A spacious sun parlor, a roof garden and other rooms designed for rest and relaxation were also among the newly planned features. Conveniently located near the heart of downtown Cleveland, this hotel was particularly well equipped for convention groups, banquets and dances.

Cleveland was to be the seventh "bachelor hotel" (or "club residence") in the Allerton Hotel chain. Five of the hotels were located in New York and one on the miracle mile in Chicago. A "bachelor hotel" was focused on the permanent male resident rather than guests visiting Cleveland. As noted by the general manager of the facility at the time, D.J. Martin, "Filling a residential hotel is a slower process than getting under way with one that caters to transients. Applications for rooms are thoroughly investigated. Every reference given is communicated with. Our policy is to rent from week to week. We neither give nor ask for long-term leases."[8]

In the mind of the Allerton Hotel management, it had put the eloquent "club" life within the reach of bachelors on a one-room budget. As the Allerton was being launched in Cleveland, it heavily advertised the hotel as the place where a bachelor could "live in 9 rooms and only pay for one." The Allerton promoted itself as a "club residence," which was copied from the company's Chicago and New York hotels, where young men or male travelers could use the hotel. The Allerton's original architectural plan included a modified "E" design and would include 530 rooms, 200 of them with private baths. The land for the hotel was leased for ninety-nine years at a $25,000-a-year flat fee.

However, between the time the hotel was announced for development and when it was actually built, the Allerton chain made a significant social change by allowing women to stay at the hotel. It seems there were not enough "bachelor" men in Cleveland. And certainly if women were allowed to stay (on designated floors), more men might stay at the hotel. When the Allerton was officially opened, the "bachelor hotel" reserved four floors for women only. Floor clerks were hired to make sure that no "stags" were found on these floors. The rich American walnut with wainscoting would have smote any patron, male or female, walking into the lobby. Immediately off the lobby was a cigar stand, the main office desk, a mailing room, a porter's room and public, as well as house, telephone booths.

Retail stores were planned for the ground floor along the East Thirteenth Street area. The Allerton offered a large street-level cafeteria, available to the public, built along the Chester Street side. The main dining room was constructed on the second floor above the cafeteria, although both shared a common kitchen. The main office and lobby were also at street level with a grand three-door entrance on the East Thirteenth Street side. A short walk to the south of the Allerton would bring the guests of the hotel to the Sterling & Welch, Higbee Company and Halle Brothers department stores, as well as the Cowell & Hubbard jewelry store (today a dynamic restaurant of the same name operated by Chef Zack Bruell.) A quick left turn on Euclid Avenue from East Thirteenth would bring the hotel guest to the grand theaters of Playhouse Square—the Allen Theater, Ohio Theater, State Theater and the RKO Palace Theater.

The street-level cafeteria was called the Coffee Shop, and it occupied the corner on Chester Avenue at the west end of the building. There was a small lobby that connected the main lobby of the hotel to the shop. It could accommodate 150 persons at a time—50 at the counter and the other 100 at tables. The real stunner was the operating hours of the shop—7:00 a.m. to 2:00 a.m. every day. Nearby the Coffee Shop was the Allerton Drug Company. It was managed by S.B. Berman and was a copy of the Ambassador Drugstore in Atlantic City.

Additional features in the original design included a sun porch for use in the winter and an open garden for use in the summer, both located on the roof. A large lounge on the top floor was also available. This fabulous bar was popular with the newspaper crowd, including reporters and editors for the *Plain Dealer*, the *Press* and the *Leader*. The room was full of politicians and business barons looking to sell stories or eavesdrop to hear the rumors, or facts, of the day. The rooftop solarium was a heavily trafficked area during the hotel's early days. It was full of small, intimate tables. Afternoon tea was served, and numerous random dance parties were known to continue into the wee hours of the morning. The roof garden opened in the spring of 1927 with Harold Ortli and his Allerton Orchestra. A featured singer that evening for the orchestra, Violet Lucille Whipple, ended up living in the old hotel, as it was later renamed Park View Apartments.[9] The papers reported the opening event for the solarium being "packed with college students."

A billiard room was open for business, as well. In a connected three-story wing on the Chester Avenue side, there resided a full gymnasium, six squash courts and a full-sized swimming pool. The hotel even offered its guests a championship-sized tennis court with a complete illumination system especially designed by General Electric. At the time, the tennis court at the Allerton was one of only four indoor tennis courts of regulation size in the downtown area of Cleveland. It was also in this unique annex that the "club rooms" for college clubs and fraternities would be located. The Allerton was the quirky mix of hotel, small privileged apartments and private male clubs. Prices for the larger suites with bathrooms were twenty dollars a week; rooms with communal restrooms were priced at ten dollars a week with a few rooms offered at lower rates.

The swimming pool offered a unique set of dining and entertainment selections. A patron of the Allerton could have breakfast or luncheon parties in the swimming area. At dinnertime, guests could be served at the tables at the side of the pool or, if they chose, could eat dinner from floating tables in the pool! The pool was well appointed architecturally and was beautifully finished. The swimming pool was immediately west of the main lobby and down a couple of steps. It was a welcoming sight for tired bachelors to be sure. The pool was sixty by twenty-five feet. It was nearly ten feet deep at one end and four and a half feet deep at the other. As noted in the hotel's marketing materials, "It is one of the most beautiful pools and rooms in the country, finished in many colors, with statuary in a niche at one end. At one side of the pool is a visitors' platform large enough to seat fifty persons at tables."

There was an annex constructed above the visitors' platform in the pool. The mezzanine housed a Turkish bath area with showers, steam rooms and massage equipment. The basement, too, offered a unique set of amenities, which included a barbershop, the well-appointed billiard room and a "Closet Club." The "Closet Club" was an Allerton Hotel creation. Each hotel in the chain had its own club. And it was literally a closet rental where a gentleman could store his tuxedo or an extra suit or two. The fee was two dollars for a year and the "club" had a couple of valets who would dry clean the suit and have it ready for the wearer. One did not even have to rent a room at the hotel to be a part of the "Closet Club."

It was on the second floor of the hotel where the Allerton really began to assume its place as a "bachelor's hotel" or "club hotel." The second floor served as the main gathering place for guests. The floor was well served with card rooms, the main dining facility and a big assembly room and dance hall. A section of the second floor was set off with its own private lobby for the Big Ten Club, a private club at the time catering to male graduates.

The Big Ten Club was the first tenant to sign a lease at the new Allerton Hotel. The club leased rooms on the second floor across the front of the building (East Thirteenth Street side), which included a lounge, a lobby, a reading room, a dining room and club offices. The members of the Big Ten Club also had liberty to make use of any other features of the hotel, and members of the club were quite fond of the roof garden, large banquet hall and swimming pool. The Allerton employed a Fraternities secretary who would arrange for members of college fraternities to meet at the hotel. At the disposal of the Fraternities secretary was the Fraternities Room, which was a large lounge room with a piano.

Access to the second floor was by elevator or by a grand staircase, which led two ways from a dramatic landing. The second-floor main lobby was almost as big as the first floor. On the south side of the second floor was a grand ballroom. The Cleveland Advertising Club, the first of its kind in America, had offices along the entire third-floor side looking over Chester Avenue.

The club's offices included a dining room as well. The Cleveland Advertising Club officially opened beautiful new quarters in the Allerton Hotel on April 13, 1927, when a debate on "Debt Cancellation" between Congressman Theodore E. Burton and Sir George Paisch, a famous British economist, was featured.[10] The club had been headquartered in the basement of the Hotel Statler prior to its new digs at the Allerton. The wishes of the membership were to afford an office space above ground.

As the newest grand hotel of Cleveland, the Allerton Hotel had to build a rich, luxurious event baronial ballroom for its guests. It was a massive room located on the second floor of the building. The hall could seat between seven and eight hundred diners. If a stage was required, the hotel was equipped with a portable stage that could be set up on quick notice. It, just like the lobby, was decked out in American walnut and a high wainscoting along the walls. The ballroom floor was a "worm eaten cherry"—or rather an imitation of such. The ceiling was "groined and beamed and here again is to be seen wainscoting which lends hominess to the place despite its great size." The room was so large that members of the Big Ten Club had taken to calling the ballroom the "tennis court." Not just because the room was large—it was enormous—but rather due to the fact that there were no columns or obstructions in the vast room. The ballroom used a special type of lighting that was hidden in niches along the ceiling, concealing the lights. Of course, engineers from General Electric at Nela Park had developed this unique lighting method and won great acclaim for doing so.[11]

The Allerton Hotel selected land that was widely considered strategic given that little space was available on Euclid Avenue for a hotel. The land itself has a rich history of its own. It was originally a part of a significant tract of land owned by Samuel Mather. Mather was one of Cleveland's wealthiest citizens and owned the Cleveland Iron Mining Company. This parcel was then part of a larger piece of land that extended along East Thirteenth Street south to (and including) the site of the Higbee Company building. Allerton signed a lease with an annual fee of $17,300 and required that a building be constructed on the property by 1923. Amendments were made to the lease and extended to match the Allerton construction schedule. Prior to the Allerton's being built, the site at one time was an old Higbee Company property. The more famous Higbee department store, which is now the Horseshoe Casino, was built at Terminal Tower by the Van Sweringen brothers near the Hotel Cleveland.

What was interesting at the time of the Allerton Hotel announcement that it was building in Cleveland was the fact that East Thirteenth Street had not been extended past Superior Avenue as of yet. Chester Boulevard was being considered for a grand extension to the East End park system across Wade Park and connecting with Euclid Avenue in Uptown, or what is known as University Circle today. Also being debated by civic leaders at this time was a possible subway along Euclid Avenue. When that was discarded as being improbable, Chester Boulevard was thought of as the next-best place to build the subway. The starting location for the subway was to be Wade Park, which would then follow Chester into downtown with a planned stop at the Allerton. Had either subway system been constructed, the fortunes of the Allerton might have been much different.

It was noted heavily in the press at the time of the Allerton's opening that the hotel would be introducing a new sport to the Cleveland masses: squash. Squash was a well-known and enjoyed game by the East Coast elites, but it had never made an appearance in Cleveland. Upon the hotel's opening, general manager D.J. Martin explained why the hotel chain was sure the sport was about to make a vibrant splash in Cleveland: "Squash too will become a favorite indoor sport here, we believe. In our hotels in the east this [squash] room is engaged almost every hour of the day and at night as well."

Before assuming his role as general manager, D.J. Martin had been in Cleveland for over a year and a half supervising the construction and furnishing of the grand hotel. Originally from New York City, Martin had been a star in the hotel chain's management. Martin had spent six years in the company's New York operations and was finally given a chance to build the Cleveland facility. It was a position for which he had been well groomed by the company to assume.

During his time managing the construction of the facility, Martin took time to meet with trade associations and individuals to improve the hotel's social contacts. He was also savvy enough to know that, to make a real splash with the Cleveland natives, the management team associated with the hotel had to be from Cleveland. A Miss Helen Smith was named as secretary to the management. Mrs. Amy Bowman, well known in Cleveland society circles and a name du jour in the society pages, was promoted as the manager of the women's department. Frank Brady, who had earned his management stripes at the famed Hotel Hollenden in Cleveland, was named manager of the porters. And a Mrs. Cole, native Clevelander, was the manager of the kitchen, dining room and banquet services. Ray Watts, a well-known coach at Otterbein College and West Tech High School, was named the recreational director of the hotel.

The furnishings of the Allerton Hotel made the news, too. A *Plain Dealer* headline at the time of the hotel's opening screamed, "Allerton Is Distinctive in Furnishings." Since the Allerton was designed in a northern Italian architectural style, the idea was to use Italian-designed chairs made of dark brown wood brightened up a bit with brass trimmings and covered in rich, red plush mohair. As noted in the same *Plain Dealer* article, "Those of the easy types [of chair] are of various designs, including Charles of London, Old Colony Club, Princeton, Lawson and high back formal."

Many of the tables in the hotel were handmade of dark oak imported from Germany. The table lamps were imported from Japan. Northern Italy, again, had supplied center lamps and many ornaments and decorations for the lobby. The floors in the lobby and on the room floors were made of terrazzo. The Allerton Hotel chain wanted every lobby and every room in its properties to look like the others so that any guest or visitor would recognize it instantly. No matter where one traveled, there was comfort to be had at the Allerton.

It was in early 1930 when the Allerton Hotel Company relinquished management of the building to the Knott Company, although the chain retained ownership. The segregation of men and women by floor was discontinued, and the hotel focused on convention business. Shortly thereafter, the Allerton Company took back the management of the building and, in 1936, falling victim to the Great Depression, filed for bankruptcy protection. That same year, a number of local investors, using the Cleveland Allerton Hotel Inc. legal structure, acquired the building and changed the operation to a full-service hotel, thus competing with the traditional hotels in downtown like the Statler and Hollenden. The "club residence" concept of the Allerton Hotel was forgotten.

THE COMINGS AND GOINGS AT THE ALLERTON HOTEL

While the Allerton does not enjoy the rich stories of the Hotel Hollenden, Hotel Statler or even the Hotel Cleveland, a number of unique historical tidbits did, in fact, occur there. The Allerton was always vying for second-class citizen status with the other hotels. And it never really occupied a good strip of real estate to make it the best hotel in Cleveland. Still, parts of its history are fantastic and fun.

Cleveland's venerable radio station WTAM pioneered the first live broadcast from a dirigible airship in 1926. A Goodyear blimp carefully navigated itself over downtown Cleveland coming west along Chester Avenue and then hovering over the Hotel Allerton. The captain of the airship sweated out each gust of wind coming off Lake Erie. Guests and residents of the hotel either stood on the roof or craned their necks from the windows of their rooms. There was a massive crowd standing along East Thirteenth Street and Chester Avenue watching this massive blimp drop radio lines to the engineers of WTAM standing on the roof of the hotel. The engineers then created a live broadcast of an ongoing conversation between the dirigible, the WTAM studio and the Goodyear plant in Akron.[12]

During World War II, the Allerton made a pleasant home for WAVES (Women Accepted for Voluntary Emergency Service) stationed in Cleveland.[13] The navy took over the hotel in 1944 as a barracks house for one thousand WAVES. The third floor was converted to an infirmary and the ballroom to a mess hall. The cocktail lounge was closed. In 1946, the navy transferred the hotel back to its civilian owners.

The Coffee Shop at the Allerton Hotel, hoping to bring in its own entertainment, experimented with a small stage concept. Dubbed the Café Miniature, it was a small, intimate stage. The inaugural house band was the "Three Musketeers," a Cleveland trio composed of Ernie Taylor, Claud Haughland and Willie Potts.

Starting in the early 1950s, the Allerton Hotel launched the Ring Theater. The theater was built on top of the hotel's swimming pool. Numerous plays and musical acts performed at the Ring Theater. But the competition for downtown entertainment was quite rich then, and the Ring Theater lasted only a few seasons, much to the delight of swimming enthusiasts.

The Waning Years

In 1943, the Hotel Allerton converted all its third-floor parlor rooms to fifty additional guest rooms. The new capacity of the hotel was six hundred rooms. After a brief period of time during which the navy commandeered the hotel, the Allerton enjoyed some good years financially. Another major remodeling for the hotel was announced in 1952 and reduced the number of rooms by converting a number of single rooms into double rooms. In 1953, the Allerton was sold to the Manger Hotel Chain for $2.4 million—a curious figure since the original hotel was built for $2.5 million. But it spoke to the type of guest the hotel was now attracting. The new management further reduced the number of rooms to four hundred total.

The financial condition of the hotel became very precarious in 1966. Facing a financial disaster, officials at the Manger Hotel begged Cleveland State University to buy the hotel for use as a dorm. The owners of the Manger complained about the competitive landscape of Cleveland and how occupancy rates were the lowest of any major city. Facing a desperate situation, the Manger Hotel chain sold the hotel to a local group of investors for $2 million in 1970.[14] The name of the hotel was again changed, this time to the Gaslight Inn. On May 27, 1971, the bar and restaurant employees of the Gaslight Inn were notified that the kitchen operations of the hotel would close that day forever. Management did notice an uptick in room bookings and banquet opportunities, but that was due to the tragic fire at the Pick-Carter Hotel (Winton Hotel) earlier in the year. The good fortune was temporary, and everyone—from the general manager to the bellboy—knew it. The hotel did not have the rents from the Big Ten Club or the Cleveland Advertising Club anymore. By this point in the hotel's history, it was renting a few small offices, and the downtown Elks Club had a few rooms. The hotel had fifty permanent guests, many of whom were nervous about whether they would remain there if the hotel closed.

Park View Federal Savings & Loan Association announced on May 14, 1971, that it would recommend foreclosure of the hotel to a judge due to an outstanding loan of $825,000 that had not been paid on by the Gaslight Inn. This essentially was the last nail in the coffin for the Gaslight, formerly the Allerton. On May 28, 1971, it was officially announced that the hotel would close. The gym building constructed along Chester Avenue was torn down, and in its place, a parking garage was constructed. The building received new life as housing for the elderly and then Section 8 housing. In 2006, the building was given a $16 million facelift but remained low-income housing. All the former amenities have been ripped from the building over the years. Today, the former Allerton Hotel is known as the Parkview Apartments. The building retains a regal look, a blessing from its glorious past, but anyone walking by it today would never get the feeling that the Allerton Hotel was once considered a grand hotel in Cleveland.

Above: Aerial view of the rooftop gardens and solarium at the Allerton Hotel. *Photo courtesy of the* Cleveland Press *Archives.*

Left: A spectacular entrance for the Allerton Hotel on East Thirteenth Street. *Photo courtesy of the* Cleveland Press *Archives.*

The Allerton Hotel stands proudly among the hustle and bustle of the Sixth City. *Photo courtesy of the* Cleveland Press *Archives.*

A couple of "bunnies" watch a boxing match at the Allerton Hotel. *Photo courtesy of the* Cleveland Press *Archives.*

The Allerton Hotel possessed a marvelous hotel lobby in the 1960s. *Photo courtesy of the* Cleveland Press *Archives.*

Female guests enjoy a cool dip in the Allerton pool. *Photo courtesy of the* Cleveland Press *Archives.*

Opposite, top: Guests take in the views on the Allerton rooftop bar. Terminal Tower illuminates the background. *Photo courtesy of the* Cleveland Press *Archives.*

Left: Another view from the rooftop bar and restaurant at the Allerton Hotel. *Photo courtesy of the* Cleveland Press *Archives.*

Above: Mary Lou Siegal, a resident of the hotel, sings with the house orchestra at the annual holiday party in 1938. *Photo courtesy of the* Cleveland Press *Archives.*

REGISTRATION

Opposite, top: The cashier and registration windows at the Allerton Hotel. *Photo courtesy of the* Cleveland Press *Archives.*

Opposite, bottom: Another fantastic view of the Allerton Hotel lobby. *Photo courtesy of the* Cleveland Press *Archives.*

Above: Spectators view a Goodyear blimp (out of frame) above as the Allerton Hotel takes part in a radio world record in 1926. *Photo courtesy of the Cleveland Public Library.*

Right: The Allerton as the Manger Hotel. All contents are for sale in 1970. *Photo courtesy of the Cleveland Public Library.*

HOTEL HOLLENDEN

One of the first hotels in Cleveland to be built east of Public Square was the Hotel Hollenden. In mid-March 1885, an advertisement in the *Cleveland Leader* declared that the Hollenden—a "new hotel on the European Plan"—would be open for business early in April. At the time of the announcement, the Stillman Hotel and its newest brethren, the Hotel Hollenden, were the only important hotels east of the square.[15] The Stillman would soon close. There was great risk, at the time, in building a hotel so far away from Public Square.

A proud banner bearing two words, "The Hollenden," flew from the tower of Cleveland's newest hotel on June 7, signifying its opening. Liberty E. Holden, one of the original owners of the hotel and publisher of the *Plain Dealer*, recognized the great need for high-grade apartment facilities. And in the Hollenden, the city had the first large hotel for transients, as well as accommodations for permanent residents. Holden had purchased the Philo Chamberlain property, fronting on Superior, Bond and Vincent Streets, to carry out his plans. Electric lights, one hundred private baths and fireproof construction—all novel features at the time—added to the Hollenden's fame. George F. Hammond, architect, designed much of the interior. For reasons lost to history, Holden reluctantly consented to provide a dining room. It was the right choice. Politicians claimed it and made it famous as a meeting place. "Hanna Hash," Mark Hanna's favorite dish, originated here. The Superior Avenue hostelry took its name from an early English form of the name Holden. In the Gay Nineties, it was the scene of colorful balls and festivities. Its bar was the longest in town.[16]

The Hotel Hollenden was a glamorous, brawny and historic building in Cleveland. Its stories are legendary, and no other hotel in Cleveland could ever live up to it. Five presidents were guests. A Cleveland "president maker"—Marcus Hanna—held court at the Hollenden daily while in Cleveland. It was the home of the most powerful African American entrepreneur in Cleveland, George Myers. The Hollenden did not witness history in Cleveland. The hotel was an active participant in making history for this great city. It was also a scene of a "rather messy gangster shooting" outside its Vincent Avenue entrance. City hall was just a short distance west of the Hollenden, on Superior Avenue near Public Square; the old courthouse was directly on the square; and there were several newspapers grouped nearby. These fed the hotel a steady patronage of politicians, lawyers, newspapermen and athletes who were the talk of the town. The Hollenden was the center of the downtown social scene.[17]

The stunning building was completed and opened in the summer of 1885, and the hotel was an immediate success. In 1886, a stock company was formed to raise money to fulfill plans to build additional rooms onto the original structure. The stock company in its entirety consisted of Jephta Wade, William J. Gordon, C. Bulkley, Stevenson Burke and Liberty Holden. It was a "who's who" list of the Cleveland elite. The grand hotel occupied the site on the southeast corner of Superior Avenue and Bond Street (East Sixth Street). Today, the Fifth Third Bank Building stands on the same plot of land.

A number of additions and renovations were made over the years, but the original building was a massive eight-story block with open ground-floor bays. There were also ranks of protecting bay windows at the center and the end of each façade. The great pyramidal roof, which rose from the corner, gave an eclectic chateau-like appearance to an otherwise modern building. George F. Hammond, a young Boston architect who moved to Cleveland at the time of this commission and later planned some of the city's more important buildings, designed the Hollenden.[18] Hammond also designed the Electric Building at 700 Prospect Avenue, the Gillsy Hotel and the five original buildings—Lowry Hall, Merrill Hall, Cartwright Hall, Kent Hall and one other structure—at the Ohio State Normal College, now named Kent State University.

A quirky feature of its original architectural plan was the construction of the building into three distinct sections. The primary section was for transient guests then traveling through the big city. The second section was for permanent residents who would live in the hotel. (Permanent residents were quite common for hotels back then and offered a monthly revenue base.) The third section was for hotel workers and all the hotel services and mechanicals. This final section was actually contained in its own building and segregated noise and odors from the living sections of the Hotel Hollenden. All sections were fireproof.

The hotel was lighted by an electrical plant and originally offered guests 420 rooms, 100 of which had private bathrooms. The hotel offered both an American plan (a room with restroom) and a European plan (room without a restroom). But most of its rooms until much later were of the European plan. Its massive lobby and publicly accessible areas were dominated by mahogany and redwood. Each room had handmade furniture, and the hotel's famed "crystal" dining room added allure to its already settled reputation for quality. Five presidents of the United States—McKinley, Taft, Theodore Roosevelt, Wilson and Harding—dined well under the ornate chandeliers of the Crystal Room, as did many famous singers, actors, diplomats and royalty.

Upon entering the large lobby off Superior Avenue, a visitor was transported to a luxurious oasis from the ever-increasing street noise. The lobby had a high-beamed ceiling with molded cherry wood and side wainscoting. At the far end opposite the entrance, a clerk's massive redwood desk crossed the entire lobby with a matching clock on the south wall. The spacious lobby had no center enclosure but instead offered guests deep, large floor carpets and lounges along the wood-paneled walls. The lobby's reception area was thirty-six feet wide, sixty-nine feet long and twenty-eight feet high and was known as one of the most impressive hotel lobbies in America. The lobby offered no stores or arcades near it but did provide a cigar counter near the Bond Street (East Sixth Street) entrance. There was also a writing room and library near the Superior Avenue entrance.

The dining rooms were on the lobby level, but the banquet hall was up a main stairway. It measured forty feet wide by seventy-two feet long with a twenty-two-foot paneled ceiling beamed with mahogany. Near the back of the banquet hall was an orchestra stand. This would later become the famous showboat room.

In 1889, a stately stone portico with an observation balcony was built over Superior Avenue, Cleveland's first outside eating area. The architectural design of the hotel was so strong that the first announced redesign of the Hollenden did not occur until 1925, when a $5 million new construction and improvement plan was initiated. The design of the new façade and architectural plan of the building was handled by the world-renowned architects Walker & Weeks. And the general contractor on the building was Craig-Curtiss Co. The 1925 redevelopment of the Hotel Hollenden included replacing the old five-story building on Superior Avenue with a new, bold twelve-story structure. The construction of the new Hollenden also included three additional shops and a two-hundred-car garage in the rear with a stunning entrance from Vincent Avenue. An additional 250 rooms were added. The Crystal Room was enlarged as well.

A second expansion was announced in 1939. This new $4 million expansion added new floors to the Hotel Hollenden, and all told, 500 new rooms were added. A new curved Short Vincent Street corner was added to the hotel as well. The hotel offered nearly 1,050 rooms for use when the 1939 expansion was completed. The *Plain Dealer* noted after the expansion that "[the Hotel Hollenden] remains one of the ornamental buildings of the city."

In 1926, a Chicago real estate company purchased control of the famous Hotel Hollenden from the Hollenden Corporation, but management eventually returned to Cleveland. Ben Tobin, who once owned the Empire State Building, purchased the historic hotel in 1945, and Alexander P. Spare of the board of trustees began operating it. In November 1946, the Hollenden, one of the country's leading commercial hotels, had its face washed for the first time since the 1926 expansion and the rejuvenating measure disclosed "a complexion of white and beautiful terra cotta."[19]

In December 1952, there was a blast in the basement of the hotel when Illuminating Company electricians were working on a high-voltage vault. By 1958, the physical structure of the Hollenden was in great disrepair, so much so that the owner at the time, Ben Tobin, would stay at the Hotel Statler. At that point, whole floors of the hotel had been abandoned.

The final owner of the Hollenden, the 600 Superior Corporation, purchased the facility in 1960. There were some plans for the remaking of the Hollenden, but by 1962, only 350 of the 1,000 rooms were in use. The 600 Superior Corporation, along with James M. Carney, announced a new fourteen-story Hollenden House hotel. The new hotel with an attached parking garage was opened in March 1965. The new Hollenden was an undistinguished architectural mess and never quite matched the legacy of the Hotel Hollenden. The Hollenden House was closed in 1989. Later that year, a Cleveland real estate developer purchased the site, and the Bank One Building, now the Fifth Third Bank Building, was constructed. The new bank building was dedicated in 1992.[20]

THE MAN THEY CALLED LIBERTY HOLDEN

He was born, as most of the Cleveland elites were at the time, somewhere else. Liberty Emery Holden was born on June 20, 1833, to Liberty and Sally Holden in Raymond, Maine. Liberty was a bit of a prodigy and was teaching at age sixteen. He then completed two years of higher education at Waterville College before moving to Ann Arbor, Michigan, to attend the University of Michigan. After graduating from "that school up North," Liberty settled into a professor position at Kalamazoo College. It was there that he became quite smitten with Delia Bulkley, and they soon married. In 1860, he was asked to become the superintendent of the Tiffin, Ohio public schools, a position he immediately accepted. He was possessed by a personal drive and wanted a better life for Delia and himself.

In 1862, Holden was accepted to law school in Cleveland, and while he tended to his studies, he began to invest in real estate as a part-time pursuit. Like many other driven and educated men in Cleveland during this period, his interests started to become quite expansive. By 1873, Holden had significant investment interests in mining properties, especially iron and silver. In 1884, Holden built the Hotel Hollenden. Originally intended as the city's first apartment house, the place became instead Cleveland's leading commercial hotel. By this time, Holden had become a leading figure in the community as a scholarly man of business and a civic-minded citizen who could always be counted on to help sponsor any movement for the city's betterment.[21]

It was December 15, 1884, when Holden, along with Charles Bukley and Roman Holden, purchased the *Plain Dealer*. The newspaper business was highly competitive in Cleveland. The citizens of the Sixth City could read the *Plain Dealer*, the *Herald*, the *Press* or the *Leader*, not to mention the various foreign language dailies printed for the numerous immigrants now calling Cleveland home. Pressured to compete with a morning edition, Holden and his other investors acquired the *Herald* in 1885 so that they could publish morning, evening and Sunday editions.[22] By 1905, Holden had abandoned the evening edition, and the *Press* then became the lone evening paper for Cleveland.

Holden proved to be a great steward of the *Plain Dealer*. He assured readers that "we shall at all times be watchful of the right man, holding that man is superior to party and that all government should be for the good of the governed." He was masterful at business and saw in Cleveland a perfect place to seize opportunity and to live the American dream. However, his dream almost became a part of the ash heap of history when, in 1908, the *Plain Dealer* building, located on the northwest corner of East Sixth

Street and St. Clair Avenue, burned to the ground. Temporary quarters had been established in the abandoned livery stable of the Hotel Hollenden on Superior Street adjacent to the hotel itself. Into these cramped quarters moved the editorial department. In them was set up a battery of new linotype machines. "Here new stream tables were put in operation making the matrices, which were sent across the street to the stereotype machines and presses operating in the basement of the burned structures."[23] Holden was the calm in the storm, and out of this near tragedy, he strengthened the position of the *Plain Dealer* in the local newspaper market.

Holden was very proud to call Cleveland home and was engaged in numerous civic projects. He was largely responsible, as president of the building committee, for the construction of the original Cleveland Museum of Art, as well as Wade and Rockefeller Parks. He eventually became president of the Union Club and served as mayor of Bratenahl.[24] He passed away quietly on August 26, 1913. Upon his death, his ownership interests in the *Plain Dealer* were transferred to his heirs.

THE MOST POWERFUL BARBER IN THE UNITED STATES

George Myers was a humble but proud man who, despite racism and fighting stereotypes of the day, became one of Cleveland's first African American entrepreneurs and a powerful political activist. Myers was born into a blue-collar life in Baltimore. His strong-willed and principled father worked at the Inner Harbor shipyards as a caulker but also became the president of the black wing of a national labor union. Myers learned how to fight for his civil rights from his father, and the lessons learned in Baltimore served him well many years later in Cleveland.

After being denied entrance into a college in Baltimore, Myers decided to learn the barber trade. After a few years as an apprentice in Baltimore, he moved on to greener pastures in Cleveland. In 1879, Myers found employment at the Weddell House Barbershop. The Weddell House was a nationally famous building sitting on the corner of Superior Avenue and Bank Street (now West Sixth). The Weddell House opened in 1847 and offered over two hundred rooms to be used as offices, stores, parlors, dining areas and overnight lodgings in addition to housing a tavern and a barbershop.[25] In 1861, President Lincoln gave an address from a second-story balcony overlooking Superior Avenue to an adoring crowd below.

Myers worked diligently at the Weddell House Barbershop for nine years and became accustomed to grooming politicians, actors, authors, opera singers and many other famous persons. It was during this time that Myers met two individuals who would have a profound influence on his life. The first was a powerful politician, known to many as the "president maker," Marcus Hanna. And the second person was Liberty Holden, the publisher of the *Plain Dealer* and the new owner of the Hotel Hollenden.

In 1888, Holden sought out Myers to become the owner of the Hollenden Barbershop. Myers was quite humbled by the offer but had no real personal money to acquire the barbershop. Nonetheless, Holden and a few of his friends put up the money to ensure that Myers would become the new owner. This was a monumental life change for Myers. The clientele of the Hollenden Barbershop was a "who's who" of local politicians, industrialists and financiers. No fewer than eight presidents and cultural luminaries, such as Mark Twin, took turns in his chair. It became a "mark of distinction" to have a personal shaving mug on Myers's own rack.[26] Of course, Myers's favorite client and good friend was "Uncle Mark," as he affectionately called Hanna.

Hanna undoubtedly saw a political win by having Myers as a member of the Republican Party. And Myers was eager to join "the game," if only to support his good friend. Myers was named a delegate to the 1891 state delegation, helping William McKinley become Ohio's governor. Myers, with Hanna's support, began organizing black delegates for the GOP in Ohio, Louisiana and Mississippi. Later, Myers was named to the Ohio Republican Party's state executive party. There were few African American Republicans more powerful than the barber from Cleveland. During his participation in Republican politics, Myers was offered many political appointments but always decided to stay with "his family" at the barbershop.

At its zenith, the Hollenden Barbershop employed thirty-five people, including seventeen barbers, six manicurists, five porters, three hairdressers for the female clients, two cashiers and two podiatrists.[27] Myers built the most technologically advanced barbershop in the United States and took great pride in that fact. One of his prized innovations was the available telephone at each barber's rack just in case his powerful clientele needed to make a hasty phone call.

Myers's influence in Republican politics began to wane after Hanna's surprise death in 1904. The civic-minded barber would still fight for many righteous causes, including demanding equal access for the African American community to the city's hospital and medical facilities. This issue was cemented into law in 1930, when the Cleveland City Council voted to open the city hospital to all races.

Unfortunately, Myers's last fight for equality involved his own barbershop. Since its opening in 1888, the Hollenden Barbershop employed only African American barbers, affording them a middle-class lifestyle. In the late 1920s, new ownership of the hotel was pushing Myers to fire his staff and hire white barbers. He refused but knew as soon as he sold his business, the new owners of the barbershop would acquiesce to the hotel and would fire Myers's veteran staff. He pushed off retirement as long as he could and was beginning to develop serious health issues when, on the morning of January 17, 1930, he told his staff that before everyone left that day he needed to talk with them. During lunch, Myers went out to buy a train ticket for a well-deserved vacation when he collapsed and died in line at the train station.

Cleveland has mostly forgotten Myers, which is a terrible shame. He deserves to be remembered as a pioneer for the African American community even if his progressive politics were for the Republican Party. He was a great political mind and a shrewd businessman who literally died to ensure his barbers would retain their prized jobs. He also was an integral part of the Hollenden's being one of the most powerful and influential institutions of its day.

The Kidnapping of Billy Whitla

Billy Whitla, a kidnapped boy, was returned to his waiting father in the lobby of the Hotel Hollenden on March 23, 1909. A day later, the kidnappers, Mr. and Mrs. James Boyle were apprehended in Cleveland and confessed.[28]

A small dusty buggy rolled up to a grade school in Sharon, Pennsylvania. Inside the buggy were a husband and wife, who notified school officials they were there to pick up Billy Whitla, the eight-year-old son of wealthy parents, due to an outbreak of smallpox. Billy's father, James, was a lawyer, and Billy's uncle was steel millionaire F.H. Buhl.

The school officials gave the boy over to the couple without hesitation. The couple waved to the officials and then slowly disappeared into the Pennsylvania countryside. After stopping at the next local town, Billy was asked by the kidnappers to drop a note into a mailbox so that his mother would know where he was going. It was actually a ransom note.

The kidnappers then drove the carriage with Billy to Warren, Ohio, where the trio boarded a train to Cleveland. The letter detailed a drop of

$10,000 in ransom money to be delivered to a public area in Ashtabula, Ohio. However, the money was never picked up, and a second letter was delivered to James Whitla, which told him to deliver the $10,000 ransom to a woman in a store on East Fifty-third Street in Cleveland. After dropping off the envelope, Mr. Whitla was told to retreat to the lobby of the Hotel Hollenden and wait for his son.

After the enveloped was delivered, as instructed, the boy was led to a trolley car on the corner of Payne Avenue and East Thirtieth Street, told to board and get off at the Hotel Hollenden stop. The Cleveland police notified a handful of staff at the hotel and had plainclothes cops on the street and in the lobby with the elder Whitla. The boy actually missed his stop and, acting nervous on the trolley, was asked by the motorman where he was heading. The young Whitla told him the Hollenden. So the motorman stopped the car near Public Square and walked the boy back to the hotel.

As the motorman and the boy approached the hotel, the Hollenden's bell captain (who was one of twelve police officers and hotel staff to be in the know of the kidnapping), Prince Hunley, quickly ran up to the duo and ushered them into the lobby. Billy, upon entering the lobby screamed, "Where's my daddy?" His father scooped him up in an emotional moment.

To the relief of everyone, Billy was in good health and spirits. For the benefit of the police, the young boy had a strong memory and recalled dozens of landmarks that helped the police zero in on the hideout. The chief of police (and future mayor) Fred Kohler had nine teams of detectives on the lookout.

The very next day, the couple was caught in a saloon on Ontario Street. Why they did not leave the city for places unknown is beyond belief. The kidnappers had spent $150 on booze and food. The rest of the ransom money was found by police. Mr. Boyle got life in the big house and died in prison. His wife served twelve years and died a broken woman not two years after her release. Billy recovered well and eventually became a lawyer, like his father, but died young, at age thirty-two, from pneumonia.

THE UNTOUCHABLE AND THE HOLLENDEN

One of the more fascinating stories involving the Hotel Hollenden includes one of America's most notorious lawmen: Eliot Ness, Mr. Untouchable. Ness had received national acclaim in Chicago as the man who finally caught

Public Enemy Number One, Al Capone. While a lot of Ness's activities are more legend than truth, he was widely considered a top-notch federal agent and a first-rate publicity hound. In 1935, Eliot Ness was offered the safety director position for the City of Cleveland by then mayor Harold Burton. This position gave him the full authority over the police and fire departments for the city. It was an endeavor in which Ness would thrive.

He brought his deep-seated bravado of protecting the public with a dramatic war on the Cleveland mafia, a group that was vastly powerful, especially "Big" Angelo Lonardo, "Little" Angelo Scirrca and Moe Dalitz, among others. Ness burned the midnight oil, too, during the "Kingsbury Run Murders," which brought terrible fear to the Cleveland masses from 1935 to 1938. Unfortunately, his otherwise remarkable career in Cleveland began to slowly wither after 1938 due to a public divorce from his first wife, Edna Staley Ness, and a quick marriage in 1939 to Evaline MacAndrew. He was also gaining a well-worn reputation as a heavy drinker.

It was in March 1942 that Ness's career received its most serious setback, opening the way to his departure from the cabinet of Mayor Frank J. Lausche. One dark morning, at 4:45 a.m., Ness's car skidded and slammed into an oncoming vehicle on the West Shoreway.[29] The story could have ended there, frankly, since Ness was the safety director of the Sixth City. But for some unknown reason—perhaps panic, maybe cowardice—Ness and his wife left the scene.

Earlier that evening, the safety director, his wife and two close friends had been drinking in the Vogue Room of the Hotel Hollenden.[30] While not Ness's regular spot, which was the Bronze Room at the Hotel Cleveland, the Vogue Room was a quick jaunt from city hall on East Sixth Street. Ness was known as a boozer, and that night in March, he certainly did not disappoint. But the times were different back then, and no one seemed to question the Untouchable as he carefully opened the car door for his new wife, made sure she was comfortable and then jumped into the driver's seat and sped off into the night.

As Ness sped along the Shoreway, he lost control of his vehicle, went over the median of the west side thoroughfare (which did not have the cement barriers it has today), clipped an oncoming vehicle and then stopped for a minute or two. Ness actually ran back to the other vehicle, noticing that there had been no eyewitnesses, and asked the other driver if he was all right. After receiving a less-than-enthusiastic yes, Ness jumped into his car and inexplicably sped off. Ness evidently stopped at a nearby pay phone and, without telling the authorities who he was, reported the accident and asked the police to help the stranded motorist.

The police responded immediately and did help the whiplashed motorist by the name of Robert Sims from East Cleveland. Sims noted the license plate number to the police, who included it—EN-1—in their report. But Ness's name was not named in the filed report. The plate was very familiar to Clevelanders and especially to policemen.[31] It was the plate number of their very famous boss, Elliot Ness. Police were, obviously, curious why Ness had left the scene. Many in the police department knew of Ness's proclivity for spirits and libations, but few offered any advice or counsel regarding his vice. Sims, however, did later make statements to the press that Ness offered his assistance to him and, did in fact, identify himself as Eliot Ness. Ness noted to Sims that his wife was injured and he wanted to make sure she was OK by immediately driving to a hospital. He did not make the trip to the hospital but instead drove his wife to their home in Rocky River.

Unbelievably, Ness did not have to resign his post at the city once this event came out in the press. But the accident marked the waning influence of Ness in Cleveland. His days were numbered. Soon thereafter, Eliot Ness and his wife moved to Washington, D.C., where he took on a federal job during the war. In 1944, he returned to Ohio to become the chairman of the Diebold Corporation, then just a security safe company not the large technology and ATM conglomerate it is today. Ness returned to Cleveland to run for mayor in 1947 but lost. In 1951, he was asked to resign from Diebold.

The last years of Ness's life were a sad footnote to a dramatic career. He was forced into taking odd jobs to earn a living, including as an electronics parts wholesaler, a clerk in a bookstore and selling frozen hamburger patties to restaurants. He collapsed and died at his home in Coudersport, Pennsylvania, on May 16, 1957, at the age of fifty-four. In the months prior to his death, Ness had been collaborating with Oscar Fraley on the book *The Untouchables*, which was a highly successful novel and was the inspiration for the popular 1960s TV show of the same name. Ness returned to Cleveland in a strange, if not endearing, way in 1997, when his ashes were dispersed in Lake View Cemetery's Wade Lake.

How Dino Crocetti Became Dean Martin

Dean Martin was an amazing entertainer who held captive the ears and hearts of many around the globe. His silky soft voice sang the songs that people fell in love with for years. He was a singer at heart but a movie star, too. He was an original member of the Rat Pack. He hung out with the likes of Jerry Lewis, Frank Sinatra and Sammy Davis Jr. And later in life, he became a huge TV star with his weekly variety show and his annual roasts of other old-school stars. He was witty, dynamic and charismatic. And he got his big start at the Hotel Hollenden.

Dean Martin was born Dino Paul Crocetti on June 7, 1917, in Steubenville, Ohio, to Gaetano and Angela. His father was a successful barber in Steubenville. As a child, Dino loved to sing at family events. When he went to the Saturday movies, he would sing out loud to Bing Crosby's songs. Dino dropped out of high school around the tenth grade and became a welterweight boxer by the name of Kid Crochet. He must not have been much of a boxer because many in the industry called him Punchy.

By 1939, Dino was a dealer, roulette stickman and a croupier at Youngstown's Jungle Inn, a well-known illegal gambling parlor. His first paid singing gig was as "Dino Martini" at a dance hall above a chop suey joint in Columbus. But in 1940, he was finally hired—for the princely sum of thirty-five dollars a week—by the Sammy Watkins Orchestra. The orchestra had been the house band for the posh Vogue Room at the Hotel Hollenden. His new stage name was Dean Martin. Martin's first performance in Cleveland got a national write-up in *Variety* magazine. "Watkins has acquired a new vocalist, Dean Martin, who backs a personable kisser with a low tenor and agreeable manner."[32] He met Betty McDonald, who was traveling with her father on business, while he was singing at the hotel. They ended up marrying and buying a house in Cleveland Heights.

Meanwhile, Martin's career began to take off. The Sammy Watkins Orchestra and Martin secured a spot on a new national show on NBC radio. The group played out of the WTAM studios in downtown Cleveland. Martin began to gain national celebrity. He was itching for his big chance at stardom. So in 1943, Martin broke his contract with the orchestra and headed to New York, where he signed on with the MCA talent agency. And from there, the rest is history. But for three glorious years, Martin was the biggest thing in Cleveland. His easy style and wonderful voice made the Hotel Hollenden and its glorious Vogue Room the place to see and to be seen.

THE COMINGS AND GOINGS AT THE HOTEL HOLLENDEN

Truly, the Hotel Hollenden is deserving of its own book. The stories, legends and myths that spill out of the hotel's history are fascinating. The fledgling NFL held many owners' meetings at the Hollenden. It was the favorite hangout of politicians, royalty, movie stars, professional athletes, singers and mobsters. The following section provides just a hint of the daily comings and goings at Cleveland's premier Golden Age hotel.

The Cleveland Art Club invited the city council to attend a brilliant reception at the Hollenden on July 3, 1893, honoring Mademoiselle Rita Elandi, operatic celebrity who was appearing in Cleveland, her birthplace. Upon entering opera in her girlhood days, Amelia Groll created her stage name by Italianizing "Cleveland" into "Elandi." She enjoyed many European successes, and in Berlin, she sang for the Emperor Wilhelm.[33]

More than 125 guests attended the Cleveland Press Club banquet at the Hotel Hollenden on April 23, 1887, honoring the 323rd anniversary of Shakespeare's birth. An assembly of ladies and gentlemen heard a scholarly discourse on English literature during the days of the bard presented by J.H.A. Bone of the *Plain Dealer*. F.L. Purdy of the *Press* picked up the theme of literature after Shakespeare, and Henry A. Griffin of the *Leader* brought women of the sixteenth century to life. W.R. Rose of the *Voice* closed the speaking program in a light-hearted vein by exposing Shakespeare the humorist. "It is not probable," a newspaper report stated, "that so many active laborers on the daily and weekly press have ever come together before in this city."

In the intense presidential campaign of 1896, Ohio's William McKinley, backed and counseled by Marcus A. Hanna of Cleveland, opposed William Jennings Bryan, Democrat, the principal issues being protective tariffs and free coinage of silver. Bryan's famous declaration, "You shall not crucify mankind on a cross of gold" brought a "tremendous crush of people to see the daring orator" when he spoke from the Hollenden balcony on August 31, 1896.[34]

Legendary bartender Harry Craddock was employed as the head bartender of the Hotel Hollenden. He was hired in 1900. Craddock would end up penning *The Savoy Cocktail Book*, published in 1930. The book became a bible for mixologists. Craddock invented a number of cocktails, including the White Lady and Corpse Reviver #2, and popularized the dry martini.

The Cleveland Advertising Club was the first organization of its kind in the world, having been established on November 27, 1901, by twenty-nine men in the profession. They originally met in the old Forest City House on Public Square. The membership grew, and the club headquarters grew with it, first in the Williamson Building, then in the Hotel Hollenden and eventually in the Hotel Statler.[35]

Jacob Saperstein, the founder of American Greetings, first sold his cards in the Hotel Hollenden. From such humble beginnings, Saperstein would build what would become the largest greeting card company in the United States. Saperstein, soon after emigrating from Poland in 1905, would import greeting cards from Germany and sell them to local merchants in Cleveland, including the gift store in the Hollenden.

One of the more peculiar events to happen at the Hotel Hollenden was a double suicide that occurred on March 29, 1905. Henry L. Woodward, a New York lawyer, and Charles A. Brouse, traveling salesman from Toledo, committed suicide at the hotel during the night by shooting themselves.[36] It was tragic coincidence because the men had nothing in common besides killing themselves on the same night. No evidence was found to link the two. What is fascinating about this occurrence was that it received national attention and was written up in the *New York Times*.

On July 6, 1914, Senator Theodore Burton returned to Cleveland as a private citizen for the first time in twenty-two years. He had served in the Senate and the House under five presidents: Cleveland, McKinley, Theodore Roosevelt, Taft and Wilson. The Republican got his start in politics as a member of the Cleveland City Council. He sponsored the legislation authorizing the construction of the Panama Canal. The City Club welcomed him at a banquet in the Hotel Hollenden on July 6.[37] After retiring as a senator, Burton made a bit of political comeback by being elected to the U.S. House of Representative from 1920 to 1928. He died one day before Black Tuesday, October 29, 1929, while serving the unfinished term of Senator Frank Willis, who had died the year prior.

The wireless age got its start in Cleveland when, in 1901, inventor Lee De Forest succeeded in talking by wireless phone from the Hotel Hollenden to a team of reporters and editors on the fourth floor of the old *Plain Dealer* building. It is curious that the feat occurred in 1901 but was not reported in the paper until 1920. It was considered quite a technological feat, especially given how novel the use of radio frequencies were.

Representatives of more than twenty NFL clubs met at the Hotel Hollenden on June 24 and 25, 1922. Among many of the amendments made to the league's original charter was changing the name of the league from the American Professional Football Association to the National Football

League. It is amazing to realize that the NFL, the most powerful professional sports league in the United States, was bestowed its name in Cleveland.

Prince Nicholas of Romania visited Cleveland on November 21, 1929. The twenty-three-year-old prince spent ten hours in Cleveland as proxy for his mother, Queen Marie, who had to cancel the remainder of her American tour to return hurriedly to the bedside of her husband, King Ferdinand, who was fatally ill. Prince Nicholas visited with Romanian groups, attended church services and was honored at a dinner for six hundred at the Hollenden.[38]

The Hollenden was filled with celebrities on the evening of January 1, 1927, when radio station WJAY first went on the air. At eight o'clock, manager Charles Burns stepped to the microphone to make the opening announcement, but the generator failed, plunging the studio into darkness. Burns ran out into the street, where he appropriated twenty-two batteries from perplexed taxicab drivers, and at 9:30 p.m., WJAY made its debut.[39]

A grand Lucian feast was held at the Hotel Hollenden on May 23, 1953. A Lucian feast was a play on the Feast of St. Lucian for the first day of the twelve days of defiance, which begin the Winterval Season. The feast was a four-hour culinary banquet for forty-four lucky gourmands. It cost fifty dollars a ticket, which was a considerable sum. Dishes on the menu included terrapin soup, snails, mussels, buffalo steak, saddle of lamb and wild duck. Various vintage wines were also included.

Even late in its life, the old Hotel Hollenden still held a respectable amount of political influence. Senator John F. Kennedy paid his respect to the Hollenden. For a number of years, Senator Kennedy was a guest at a steer dinner held by Democrat powerbroker and former Cleveland mayor Ray Miller. (A quick side note on Ray Miller: he was the owner of WERE radio and is largely considered as a pioneer in rock radio.)[40] One of Kennedy's saved speeches in the American Presidency Project was given at the Hotel Hollenden just prior to his election:

> *Ray Miller, ladies and gentlemen, this is the third year in a row that I have been honored by being invited to this steer roast, and I hope that it is going to be possible for me to come back next year in a somewhat different capacity.* [Applause]
>
> *I want to say just one point about Ohio. In the 1948 election, you will recall, President Truman carried the State of Ohio by 7,200 votes. He carried Illinois by 17,000 votes, and it was the victory in this State and in Illinois which permitted him to maintain his Office of the Presidency. I think the Presidency is a great office. It is enshrined in the Constitution, and*

it also by the force of events and by the pressure of circumstances that is has come to have the greatest possible influence over the lives of us all. Therefore, as I believe that there are sharp differences between the two candidates and great issues which divide historically the two political parties, I do hope it is possible for all of you in the next six weeks to give us all the help that you can. My judgment is that the winner of this presidential election will carry Ohio, and I think it is possible for us to carry Ohio. [Applause]

It is possible for us to win Ohio, and it is possible for us to lose Ohio. My judgment is that it is a very close, tight race in this state, in Illinois, in Pennsylvania, in New Jersey and New York. These are the key States. Whoever carries these major industrial States from Illinois east quite obviously will be elected the next President of the United States.

Ohio is very important. That and Michigan and these other States must be carried by the Democratic candidate, and the Democratic Party. So I come here today asking all of you who work in the field for the party in this country, for many years, and in the State, I come here asking for your help. This election will be close, and the extra effort that you can put in this in the coming six weeks, in the next three days to get people registered, to make sure that when they are registered they come to vote, to make sure that this is not merely a contest between two names, but it is a contest between two parties and two individuals, one of whom says "Yes" to the next 10 years and the other says "No." I say, yes and I think the country says yes. [Applause]

In short, I thank you for your past help to the party, but I must say I think in 1960 the tide can rise and we can carry Ohio. Thank you. [Applause]

THE LAST DAYS OF THE OLD LADY

After living gloriously and proudly through its first sixty years, the hotel began to give way to the natural laws of physical obsolescence. Its financial position weakened by the Depression, the hotel fell into the hands of a succession of hit-and-run operators who were completely lacking in respect for the Hollenden's tradition of class and without pride in its history. Their superficial attempts at modernization spoiled the rococo splendor of the Hollenden. In a vulgar bid to prolong its earning powers, the huge chandeliers were ripped out and replaced by garish fluorescent fixtures, paint was splashed over the shining grain of the mahogany paneling, chrome-and-glass wall fixtures were installed and in places asphalt tile squares covered the old marble flooring, completing its desecration.

The stately old lady of character was turned into a gaudy frump, and when ownership finally was wrested from the hands of out-of-town interests by two Cleveland investors, James Carney and Peter Kleist, they decided it had gone too far downhill to be rescued and would have to be replaced with a new structure.[41] The demolition of the old Hollenden proved to be one of the most interesting spectacles in Cleveland. No hotel ever put up a better last-ditch fight. The wrecking company found that slamming its large iron ball into Hollenden's façade turned the ball into a misshapen mass.

After pounding the Hollenden a number of times, the ball began to look more like a cube, and the wrecker wisely turned to a slower, piecemeal system of destruction. It took him more than a year to level the structure, many months more than had been anticipated, and all admirers of this holdover from the past applauded the building's last convincing show of quality.[42]

The Hollenden House

It is fair to say that the Hollenden House was an unworthy successor of the Hotel Hollenden legacy. It was a bland concrete fabrication that spoke to what was wrong with 1960s urban Brutalism architecture. The house was a fourteen-story abomination with 350 rooms. The new hotel opened in March 1965. The Hollenden House was, and this is difficult to fathom, the first hotel to be built in downtown Cleveland in over thirty years. Built for $6 million, it was hailed as a new urban development model. It was built around the same time as the monumental Erieview redevelopment project in downtown Cleveland at East Twelfth Street and St. Clair Avenue.

The hotel received a reasonable bit of press for being the first downtown hotel to offer, for free, the Showtime cable channel. A modest renovation of the hotel took place in early 1979, when a number of the guest rooms were redecorated with new carpet, wall coverings, draperies, bedding and accessories. A health club was added in 1981, as was a new poolside bar. The house had a street-level coffee bar, the Gazette Lounge and the Sixth Street Lounge (later a Marie Scheiber restaurant).

Despite lacking the grandeur of the Hotel Hollenden, the Hollenden House carried on the political intrigue that was a common occurrence at the former hotel. It was rumored that in 1964, a number of *Plain Dealer* editors decided to risk their political capital by attempting a modest coup d'état at city hall. Ralph Locher was the fiftieth mayor of Cleveland and was widely seen as a milquetoast in political circles. The city of Cleveland in 1964 was in political and social turmoil, but few of the city's problems could move Locher to make the necessary decisions on any issue. It was as if Locher had simply bunkered down at city hall not to upset anyone as the next election approached. The "*Plain Dealer* three" (unnamed editors) decided to take matters into their own hands by reaching out to former Cleveland mayor and then U.S. senator Frank Lausche for a peculiar political favor. Meeting at the new Hollenden House in the spring of 1965 for a lunch, the three *Plain Dealer* editors asked Senator Lausche to secure a federal judgeship for Locher.[43] Lausche agreed that it was probably best for the city and immediately offered to approach Locher. Locher was taken aback by Senator Lausche's asking for an audience. Since when does a senator worry about a local mayor? But Locher did take the meeting and was even more surprised by the message. It was one of the few decisions Mayor Locher made with heavy conviction when he sternly told Lausche that he would refuse to accept any federal appointment. And with that, the mayor continued his lack of leadership at city hall. No word on what retribution, if any, was doled out to the *Plain Dealer* "treasonists."

The political intrigue continued at the Hollenden House in the early 1970s, when the *Cleveland Press* publicly urged James M. Carney, millionaire owner of the new Hollenden and longtime Democrat contributor, to run against the Republican Ralph Perk and Arnold Pickney, then president of the Cleveland school board who was running as an Independent, in the mayoral race. Perk won the election. In 1976, Howard Metzenbaum held his election night party at the Hollenden House after defeating Robert Taft for one of Ohio's Senate seats.

Social progress was made in the Hollenden House unexpectedly on April 22, 1971, when Jean Capers, an attorney, and Rosemarie Folkman demanded lunch at the "stag" Gazette Room. The men's-only lunchroom seemed worn and socially awkward, not to mention behind the times. Capers was a local attorney for the National Organization for Women (NOW). Managers of the Gazette Room purchased free beers for the ladies. The celebrated lunch (the women were photographed in the Cleveland daily papers) ended the "stag" era at the Gazette Room.

The Hollenden House did have one redeeming quality. The Hollenden Tavern, operated by Marie Schreiber, was a widely popular restaurant. Schreiber had earlier owned and operated the Tavern Chop House on

Chester Avenue before the Erieview redevelopment tore it down in 1967. She then opened a restaurant in the Hotel Statler and later at the Hollenden House. She was a grand host, well dressed with a keen eye for culinary trends.

The Hollenden House was closed in 1989.

FINAL THOUGHTS ON THE HOTEL HOLLENDEN

The Hollenden was the largest and gayest hostelry between New York and Chicago when constructed. It offered a rich nightlife for Cleveland and political intrigue for an entire nation. The Hollenden was one of the city's outstanding landmarks, a living memorial to the Victorian period. Even in the run-down condition in which it found itself at the end, it was a magnificent building, and it still enjoyed the loyalty of thousands of regular patrons who sentimentally insisted on the Hollenden address whenever they visited Cleveland.

The hotel also served as the lavish entrance to Vincent Street, or Short Vincent, once the center of Cleveland nightlife. The Hotel Hollenden was amazing in every way: the architecture, the guests, the history, the city it proudly served. No hotel in Cleveland will ever be able to match the rich, sensational history of the Hollenden. The deck is stacked against the newer hotels. What is certainly true is that no hotel should even attempt to compete with the wickedly wonderful Hotel Hollenden.

Above: A couple of fashionable ladies enjoy themselves at the Parisian in the Hotel Hollenden. *Photo courtesy of the* Cleveland Press *Archives.*

Left: The historic hotel bar at the Hotel Hollenden. *Photo courtesy of the* Cleveland Press *Archives.*

Opposite, top: The legendary Hotel Hollenden sitting on Superior Avenue and East Sixth Street. *Photo courtesy of the* Cleveland Press *Archives.*

Opposite, bottom: The hustle and bustle of the Hotel Hollenden lobby. *Photo courtesy of the* Cleveland Press *Archives.*

HOTEL HOLLENDEN

WELCOME!
BASEBALL WRITERS
OF AMERICA

Above: Restaurateur Marie Schreiber and Hollenden chef Louis Gomizal look over the hotel menu. *Photo courtesy of the* Cleveland Press *Archives.*

Left: The new owners of the Hollenden, Peter Kleist and Robert Joyce, review architectural designs of the hotel. *Photo courtesy of the* Cleveland Press *Archives.*

Right: The Hotel Hollenden days before it was to be torn down and replaced with the Hollenden House. *Photo courtesy of the* Cleveland Press *Archives.*

Below: The grand hotel being torn down. *Photo courtesy of the* Cleveland Press *Archives.*

Left: A fashionable advert extolling the virtues of the Hotel Hollenden. *Photo courtesy of the* Cleveland Press *Archives.*

Below: Coffee is served to revelers on New Years Eve at the Hollenden Garage in 1955. *Photo courtesy of the* Cleveland Press *Archives.*

The beautiful Beatrice Jones is ready to serve patrons at the Hotel Hollenden coat check. *Photo courtesy of the* Cleveland Press *Archives.*

Opposite, top: Miss Betty Booth enjoys the company of some nice lads at the Hollenden restaurant. *Photo courtesy of the* Cleveland Press *Archives.*

Opposite, bottom: The ballroom at the Hotel Hollenden. *Photo courtesy of the* Cleveland Press *Archives.*

Above: A few employees of the Hollenden Room enjoy the new "El Gaucho" room at the hotel. *Photo courtesy of the* Cleveland Press *Archives.*

Right: Wesley Brooks of the Hotel Hollenden shoe shop repairs a secretary's shoe while she waits. *Photo courtesy of the* Cleveland Press *Archives.*

A large dance at the Hotel Hollenden in February 1936. *Photo courtesy of the* Cleveland Press *Archives.*

The world-famous Showboat Theater at the Hotel Hollenden. *Photo courtesy of the Cleveland Public Library.*

Opening day trolley to the Cleveland professional baseball team. *Photo courtesy of the Cleveland Public Library.*

Cleveland versus Boston Championship Game trolley in front of the Hotel Hollenden. *Photo courtesy of the Cleveland Public Library.*

The rear of the Hotel Hollenden as taken from East Sixth Street and the corner of Short Vincent. *Photo courtesy of the Cleveland Public Library.*

Opposite, top: The crown jewel of Cleveland hotels: the Hotel Hollenden. *Photo courtesy of the Cleveland Public Library.*

Opposite, bottom: The destruction of the Hotel Hollenden. *Photo courtesy of the Cleveland Public Library.*

MO
LOA
CIGARS

Left: An original drawing of the Hotel Hollenden. *Photo courtesy of the Western Reserve Historical Society.*

Below: The view of the Hotel Hollenden from East Ninth Street. *Photo courtesy of the Western Reserve Historical Society.*

Right: The original and rather ornate Hotel Hollenden lobby. *Photo courtesy of the* Cleveland Press *Archives.*

Below: A long wait at the Hotel Hollenden. *Photo courtesy of the* Cleveland Press *Archives.*

Above: Legendary Notre Dame football players—Don Miller, Harry Stuhldreher, Jim Crowley and Elmer Hayden—enjoy their famous "Four Horsemen" photo at a Hotel Hollenden event. *Photo courtesy of the* Cleveland Press *Archives.*

Left: Rosemarie Folkman crashes the Stag Buffet at the Gazette Lounge in the Hollenden House. *Photo courtesy of the* Cleveland Press *Archives.*

Howard Metzenbaum's victory speech at the Hollenden House after defeating Senator Robert Taft. *Photo courtesy of the* Cleveland Press *Archives.*

A few ladies make their way to the Hollenden House ballroom. *Photo courtesy of the* Cleveland Press *Archives.*

Left: A mural of the Hotel Hollenden at the new Hollenden House. *Photo courtesy of the Cleveland Public Library.*

Below: Architectural designs for the Hollenden House. *Photo courtesy of the* Cleveland Press *Archives.*

HOTEL CLEVELAND

L.E. Pierce was a fastidious man overseeing Cleveland's most meticulous hotel. As general manager of the Hotel Cleveland, he had served stage and screen stars, politicians, musicians, sports figures and certainly a few gangsters. Every morning after a good cup of coffee, he would conduct his rounds of the hotel, making sure every sheet was folded just right, every carpet was clean, the priceless marble was polished just right and each dish was cleaned to a sparkling shine. He greeted all his hotel employees, who were scurrying about in front of him tasked with their chores of the day, with a quick smile and a sparkle in his eyes.

He made his way through the grand kitchen of the Hotel Cleveland inspecting the fresh produce when a back door to the kitchen was suddenly kicked in and knocked over a stack of silver trays. To Mr. Pierce's disbelief, three blue-suited men were dragging a drunk, disheveled monster of a man into the kitchen by his pant cuffs. Pierce began a series of loud objections while his stunned kitchen staff looked on in horror.

The three men were oblivious to the loud protestations of Mr. Pierce as they bickered among themselves trying to move the massive block of a man through the painfully small door. As Mr. Pierce walked closer, trying to push the men away and to lob some threats at their persons, he noticed another shadowy figure walking through the door. Mr. Pierce turned toward the man with his index finger about to point into the shadow's chest when he stopped, his jaw agape, to see one of his most famous hotel guests walk in and bark a few orders. The man was Eliot Ness, Cleveland safety director and one of the famed "Untouchables" who dared to challenge Chicago's most famous gangster—Al Capone.

Mayor Harold Burton had hired Ness in the late winter of 1935 as Cleveland's safety director. This position offered Ness a chance to manage a large city's police and safety forces. It was a task well earned by the boyish-looking Ness. As it turns out, Ness and his men had just nabbed a suspect in the investigation of the notorious torso murders and needed a venue that could keep a few secrets while he and his team questioned the suspect. Ness immediately thought of the Hotel Cleveland.

"Pierce—I apologize for the disturbance. Please call my boys at city hall," suggested Ness, "and they will offer some remuneration for your troubles."

The hotel manager was rendered mute.

"And I hate to ask, but we will need a room for our 'guest' here and my colleagues," noted Ness as he pulled Pierce by the arm. "And of course, we need to keep this matter extremely quiet from the press."

Pierce tried to collect himself, nodded approval of Ness's requests and snapped his fingers at a nearby porter.

"Take Mr. Ness and his 'party' to the freight elevator so as to not disturb our other guests," said Pierce to the porter. "And provide them every confidential amenity we can offer."

The porter nodded to his boss and motioned Ness and his unruly group to the freight elevator. Pierce shook his head for a moment trying to comprehend his morning. After a deep breath, he smiled and laughed to himself. It was just another day at the world-famous Hotel Cleveland.

WELCOME TO THE HOTEL CLEVELAND

Cutting a strong jib across the horizon of Superior Avenue, the Hotel Cleveland is an impressive piece of architecture. The hotel reflects the conservative nature of the city it serves. And with few exceptions, the Hotel Cleveland does not share the more flamboyant stories of the Hotel Hollenden or the Hotel Statler. It was the hotel, however, that all the others aspired to be. It was, and is, widely considered the "Grand Dame" of Cleveland's hotels. The Hotel Cleveland was quietly effective, a prime example of world-class service and a cunning ability to keep its rich trove of stories quite secret—although, that doesn't mean a few of its amazing stories haven't escaped.

The site where the Hotel Cleveland grandly rests has a long history of lodging and hospitality. A string of popular taverns and hotels had existed on the site since 1812. It all started when Phinney Mowrey erected his tavern on the southwest corner of Superior Street and the Public Square. It was a small log structure, situated on lot No. 82, which he had purchased from Samuel Huntington for $100 in 1812. "A spring near the log barn was a favorite meeting place."[44] One could go back even further to the original Connecticut Land Company, from which, in 1802, lot No. 82 was acquired by Samuel Huntington.

In 1820, Mowrey's Tavern was purchased by Donald McIntosh for $4,500, a princely sum at the time, and was renamed the Cleveland Hotel. The Cleveland Hotel was, unfortunately, destroyed in a fire during 1845. The property was rebuilt and then became the City Hotel. In 1848, a new building was erected and called the Forest City House. The Forest City House became the center of the city's social and commercial happenings. And outside the Weddell House, located on Superior Avenue and Bank Street (West Sixth Street), the Forest City House was the preeminent location for power brokers, socialites and men of commerce.

But times change, and by 1915, the Forest City House was antiquated. Plans, however, were in motion to build a grand hotel, a building to demonstrate the power and prestige to which Cleveland was now becoming accustomed. At midnight on August 9, 1915, the famous bar on the Public Square side of the historic Forest City House closed. The rich days of service for this famous hotel had come to an end, and on the site of Mowery's Tavern, built a century earlier, the new Hotel Cleveland was to rise. The last man to register at the old Forest City House was A.E. Castles of Oberlin. At 6:00 p.m. on September 16, the hotel concluded its business, and the sign "Closed" went on the front door. Shortly afterward, wrecking crews began tearing down the landmark.[45]

All in all, the property operated under thirteen different names through the years before it was sold to the Terminal Hotels Company on July 14, 1916. It was originally sold to John H. and Mary E. Buggie, who had planned to build on the site a beautiful one-thousand-room hotel. The mysterious and aloof Van Sweringen brothers would eventually own the plot of land. And it was they who constructed the hotel before they could assemble the rest of the land for the dramatic Terminal Tower and the Union Terminal complex.

The hotel was finished in 1918 and would eventually cost $4.5 million (in 1918 dollars) or one thousand times the outlay for the first Cleveland

Hotel that stood on the same site in 1820. L.E. Pierce, the cordial first manager, continued in charge of the dramatic hotel into the 1940s.[46] The hotel proudly displays its unique architectural shape of a large *E* resting comfortably and taking notice of all the activity unfolding along Superior Avenue and Public Square.

The renowned architectural firm of Graham, Burnham & Company designed the stunning fourteen-story Hotel Cleveland. And when completed, the building was considered one of the largest hotels in the world. Of course, no expense was spared for Cleveland's hotel crown jewel during construction. It was designed in a flattering neoclassical style with a magnificent lobby that showcases a grand staircase and marble floors with vast columns that support a vaulted ceiling of Caen stone. Decorative details captured the romantic nuances of the Italian Renaissance, including a fountain mined from the same quarry as Michelangelo's *David*.

Once inside the grand structure, a patron had all the "modern" conveniences provided for him or her. No want or desire, within reason, would go unfulfilled. The Hotel Cleveland was a cornucopia of plenty. The hotel offered a large main dining room. The beautifully designed windows of the main lobby were continued north and west to the dining area, making it one of the few naturally lighted areas in the hotel. Patrons often remarked on the snowy white linen, sparkling crystal and fine sliver.

In addition to the main dining room, the Hotel Cleveland offered the Bronze Room, which was originally located on the main floor near reception. The ceilings in the Bronze Room were much lower than in the Dining Room or the Grand Lobby. The walls were finished in a rich bronze tone, which made for a less formal atmosphere than the rest of the hotel. It was a collegial room, almost club-like in its atmosphere.

As noted in the hotel's advertising at the time: "The Ground Floor is essentially a man's domain." Beside the aforementioned Bronze Room was a modernly equipped Lunch Room offering prompt service at minimum prices. The Ground Floor Lobby and Cigar Stand, Billiard Room and Rest Room, Lavatory, Barber Shop and Chiropodist occupied the remaining space on this floor.

Also offered by the hotel were numerous private dining rooms. Another room for spirits and conversation, the Rose Room, was located near the main floor. On the mezzanine floor resided the ladies' restroom. Following a corridor past the ladies' restroom were two assembly rooms and the splendid Banquet Hall. Near the east end of the mezzanine corridor was a balcony that overlooked the main lobby and was used as a secluded and luxurious lounge. A smaller banquet room, dubbed the Georgian Room, complete with a kitchen, checking and dressing rooms, was a popular venue for club meetings or private dinners. Finally, several parlor-bedroom suites were available for official or delegation headquarters.

The hotel earned the "Grand Dame" moniker. It was a sumptuous place that spoke to its guests and offered the allure of something special and different. Few of the other Cleveland hotels could match the elegance of the Hotel Cleveland, although they all tried. And yet the hotel could have had a different architectural significance if not for curious brothers who believed the Hotel Cleveland could be an anchor for a much larger and marvelous development.

The Van Sweringen Brothers

The beautiful story arc of the Hotel Cleveland would not be complete without slipping down the rabbit hole that is the story of the Van Sweringen brothers. Rare is a rags-to-riches-to-rags chronicle about Clevelanders so dominant as the amazing tale of Oris and Mantis Van Sweringen. Within a twelve-year period (1923–35) the brothers Van Sweringen amassed a real estate portfolio that included a completed community with its own government, a rapid transit system, a transcontinental railroad that was believed to be worth between $3 to $4 billion and the construction of the largest building outside New York. And then they were broke—paupers of the Depression, victims of their own success. True to their tragic script, one of the brothers died on his personal railcar with less than $3,000 to his name. The brothers dreamed big and yet were two of the few in life to enjoy a reality much larger than what they could ever have imagined. In fact, author and *Plain Dealer* columnist George Condon once wrote of the Van Sweringen brothers: "Of all the men and women to walk the Cleveland scene over the past 170 years, O.P. and M.J. Van Sweringen did more to alter the face of the city than any other private citizens, individually or in combination. They left a deep imprint that shows no sign of eroding. They were the builders of modern Cleveland."[47]

They were of Dutch ancestry. A family member of noble birth named Gerret Van Sweringen left Holland for the New World and settled in New Castle, Delaware. The brothers were born to James and Jennie Van Sweringen near the town of Wooster, Ohio. Oris was born on April 24,

1879, while Mantis was born on July 8, 1881. The brothers were inseparable their entire life—from childhood to death. The family moved to Cleveland in 1890 for a better life, and by 1897, the brothers were working for the Bradley Fertilizer Company.[48]

Both brothers were fascinated by real estate and, by 1905, had invested in a Lakewood, Ohio development focused on Cook Avenue. The investment failed. The brothers, after a period of time operating a real estate business in their sisters' name, became real estate speculators in Cleveland Heights. It was this particular speculation that brought forth new wealth for the brothers and a bold sense of accomplishment. With newfound coin in their pockets, the brothers turned their attention to Fairmount Boulevard, a stunning avenue but with little transit options, thus limiting the area's growth potential. The Van Sweringens used their private charm on the president of the Cleveland Railway Company to extend its rail tracks and service to their new subdivision on the boulevard. It imported a mission-critical component to the Van Sweringens' future success. Every one of their developments had public transit as a central part of the plan.

Soon thereafter, the brothers acquired the desolate and moldering ruins of the North Union Shaker Community, which had fallen on very desperate times. The Shaker community was formed in the summer of 1822 as the last of the nineteen Shaker colonies. The original landholdings held nearly 1,366 acres with sixty buildings. The North Union colony became a self-supported community that grew to three hundred members by 1850.

After the Civil War, the Shaker communities witnessed declining populations in all of their colonies. It seems that celibacy was not in vogue after the War Between the States. And so by 1889, there were only twenty-seven members left of the North Union Shaker Community. A local syndicate purchased the land in 1892 for $316,000.[49] The brothers Van Sweringen bought the land for $1 million in 1905 and immediately began to develop the residential area that we now call Shaker Heights but then was know as Shaker Village. Their idea for the development was simple—build a terribly expensive, terribly exclusive and terribly desirable suburb. And in that, the brothers succeeded.

In order to transport the wealthy citizens of Shaker Heights to downtown safely, the Van Sweringens established the Cleveland Interurban Railroad. The railroad operated streetcar lines from Cleveland Heights to East Thirty-fourth Street, but the track was incomplete at this point to its intended downtown destination. So the brothers had an ingenious thought—why not purchase a railroad to complete the interurban?

It just so happens that a railroad was available for purchase. The New York Central's Nickel Plate owned land and rail tracks the brothers needed, so in 1916, they purchased the railroad.[50] This fed the brothers' belief in the importance of building a public transit amenity into their developments. The Nickel Plate transaction also started the unique financing structures the Van Sweringens used to get their ever larger and larger business transactions completed. In short order, the brothers acquired other railroads, property in downtown Cleveland and holdings in Midland Steel, Goodyear Tire & Rubber and the White Motor Company. By 1929, the Van Sweringens controlled over thirty thousand miles of railroad lines, including the Shaker Rapid Line, which was successfully finished in 1920.

Meanwhile, in 1917–18, the Van Sweringen brothers built the Hotel Cleveland on their Public Square property. On the site of the Old Forest City House, the Van Sweringens constructed the new $8 million hotel. Once the Terminal Tower was built, many years later, they designed and built another $8 million wing to house a department store and then bought the old Higbee Company to ensure a suitable tenant for the new store. This continued a trend by the brothers to acquire missing pieces of their business empire. Since they needed a department store and none would move to the new site, the Van Sweringens simply bought a department chain. A new street on stilts was built south of the department store and terminal, and on it, the Vans constructed two new skyscrapers, the Medical Arts Building and the Republic Building.[51] One of the main reasons for the conservative style was the necessity of incorporating the Hotel Cleveland of 1918 into the group. When the department store was added in 1931, its symmetrical placement required that it also be designed to match the hotel.[52]

During the acquisition of the Nickel Plate railroad, the brothers stumbled into a grand debate over Cleveland's rail terminus. Most train service at the time in Cleveland would take place at the decrepit Union Station, which was at the lakefront bluff near West Ninth Street. The other smaller train stations servicing the city were clustered in the Industrial Valley along the Cuyahoga River. These stations included the Nickel Plate, the Baltimore & Ohio, the Erie Railroad and the Wheeling & Lake Erie. The goal was to build a larger Union Station at the north end of the mall in downtown Cleveland. A bond issue was put on the ballot in 1915 and was approved by a six-to-one margin. But before any tangible building could be started, World War I broke out, and the plan was shelved.

The "war to end all wars" had unknowingly given the Van Sweringens time to contemplate and design a new Union Terminal, one that would support the Van Sweringens' new Terminal Tower project. The terminal and other new structures were planned to be constructed on the southwest corner of Public Square, which at the time was an area of high crime and squalor. In 1919, the public (enamored of the Van Sweringens' idea) voted for the redevelopment of the Union Terminal on the Public Square site, leaving the famous but competing Group Plan by Daniel Burnham forever incomplete. When the terminal project became a reality in the 1920s, the brothers decided to incorporate the Hotel Cleveland into the terminal group plan.[53]

The vast scale of this terminal development should be noted. Downtown Cleveland before or since has not seen a construction site as large or as complex. The site covered thirty-five acres of squalor that fronted on Public Square and moved westward sloping down the hill toward the Cuyahoga River. The real estate held nearly 2,200 separate buildings and housed a population of more than fifteen thousand persons.

The deconstruction of the site began in 1920 with the new Hotel Cleveland beautifully positioned along Public Square and included some of the city's most historic structures, along with the shanty shacks and eyesores. The old American House on Superior Avenue fell, as did the Central Police Station on Champlain Street, the main building of the Ohio Bell Telephone Company and the famous Stein's Café. Complete streets, too, fell victim to the development and disappeared. Champlain Street, Hill Street, Columbus Street and Diebolt Alley and its famous restaurants are forever lost to history. Portions of three cemeteries also had to be destroyed with the bodies removed and sent to various city cemeteries. Rail lines had to be rerouted to ensure that four different rail companies could use the Union Terminal, not to mention the Shaker Rapid extension.

The Union Station and Terminal Tower (including the Medical Arts Building and the Republic Building) took eleven years to complete. Actual construction began in 1923 and was finished in 1930. Estimated cost of the project exceeded $200 million. The Terminal Tower was originally planned to be fourteen stories, but the structure was expanded to fifty-two floors with a height of 708 feet and rests on 280-foot-high caissons. Designed by the firm of Graham, Anderson, Probst & White, the tower was modeled after the Beaux-Arts New York Municipal Building by McKim, Mead and White.[54]

To put it all in context, the 1930s witnessed several of the greatest undertakings in the city's history, which would influence the prestige, health and culture of Cleveland for generations. The terminal buildings were completed and were immediately rated as the second most important group of commercial buildings in the nation. A city within a city, the group embodied a tremendous railroad station, towering office buildings, Higbee's modern department store, Harvey's restaurants and shops, the famous Hotel Cleveland, a monumental post office and offices of major banks.[55]

At their financial zenith, the brothers' holdings included 231 companies with assets valued between $3 and $4 billion. Included in these properties were twenty-four railroads, real estate, coal operations and other affiliated companies. With the Van Sweringens' wealth beginning to evaporate during the Depression, *Fortune* magazine printed a story in 1934 analyzing the brothers and noted: "The Van Sweringen brothers are conveniently regarded by the business world as one man. And with some reason. For no two men of their prominence have ever so successfully merged their identities. If they had been joined like Siamese twins they could scarcely be any closer."

Real estate being the brothers' first love, it is not surprising that they enjoyed their own personal holdings as well. As part of their Shaker Heights development, the two brothers purchased a rather spectacular English Tudor at 17400 South Park Boulevard. In addition, when enjoying the spoils of downtown, the brothers called the Greenbrier Suite home. Located on the thirty-sixth floor of the Terminal Tower, the Greenbrier Suite was an amazing personal residence in a tower built for big business. The Van Sweringens also owned three luxurious private railway cars fitted with the best modern amenities at the time. But perhaps their favorite place on earth was Daisy Hill, their sprawling 660-acre expanse in Hunting Valley, just fifteen miles east of Cleveland.

Over the years, the Van Sweringen brothers had purchased four contiguous farms to create Daisy Hill. The farms lost all productivity, but the brothers found a peaceful oasis away from their growing and complex business empire. The estate included a stable, four living suites, a carpenter shop, a machine shop, twenty-two garages, a nursery, a greenhouse and a man-made lake. It took seven years to complete and cost over $3 million. When the furnishings were sold at a four-day auction sale in 1938 by the Parke Bernet Galleries, a 220-page catalogue was needed to list and describe the 1,250 items offered.[56]

The boys were not involved in any social set and frowned on being in the media. While they had national interests, they preferred to stay close to the Cleveland area. The Van Sweringens were members of the Union Club, Shaker Heights Country Club and Pepper Pike Country Club but rarely participated in the clubs' social offerings. They were best friends and inseparable.

On June 28, 1929, a formal dedication was held for the opening of the grand Tower Terminal complex, including the Hotel Cleveland, which had been built many years earlier. It was a grand celebration that included governors, senators, cabinet members and entertainers—a veritable "who's who" in the world with the exception of the Van Sweringen brothers, who decided to dine alone at Daisy Hill. It was their penultimate moment. Not four months later, the Great Depression was beginning to take form over the United States, and the Van Sweringens' vast fortunes were not immune to its effects.

The cracks started to show almost immediately in the Van Sweringens' financial empire. The main source of revenue for the Van Sweringens' conglomerate leviathan was not the real estate holdings but rather the railroad businesses. And the railroads were hit hard by the Depression. In less than two years, the Van Sweringens' railroad revenue dropped by nearly 50 percent. In the early months of 1930, the brothers turned to J.P. Morgan for financial support, and the investment bank loaned the Van Sweringens $40 million. By 1935, it was becoming evident that the loan was not going to be repaid, and an auction was called to liquidate the Van Sweringens' holdings. At the loan auction, which Oris Van Sweringen did attend, nearly $3 billion worth of assets and companies, then employing nearly 100,000 during the Depression, were acquired for $3,121,000. The new owners of the failed Van Sweringen business behemoth hired the two best individuals for the job: Oris and Mantis Van Sweringen.

Mantis began to have serious health issues in 1935 and died the morning of December 13. His brother Oris, heartbroken and lost, was quoted as saying, "I don't know what to do, or how to do it, or where to go from here." Oris lived less than a year, passing away on his personal train near Hoboken, New Jersey. It seems fitting that the brothers share a cemetery plot at Lakeview Cemetery under a tombstone that reads, "Brothers."

The two brothers were indeed the architects of the grand Cleveland that has slowly eroded over the years. But their imprint remains. Anyone walking around downtown can immediately fall under the spell of the hypnotic beauty that is the Terminal Tower and the Hotel Cleveland. But the brothers also created Shaker Heights (often considered the best planned development ever in the United States), parts of Cleveland Heights and even developed a small strip of properties in Lakewood. In addition, for a brief shining moment, the brothers were owners of the largest railroad business in the country. It is difficult to aptly describe the two men, who were so connected by the bounds of brotherhood, but perhaps the best way to detail who they might have been would come from an old Winston Churchill quote: "It is a riddle, wrapped in a mystery, inside an enigma." And of course, that would make the brothers smile.

THE COMINGS AND GOINGS AT THE HOTEL CLEVELAND

What offers character to the grand hotels of Cleveland, especially the Hotel Cleveland, is the grand march of history witnessed within and without the building's hallowed walls. The spot where the Hotel Cleveland sits is the longest continuous location of a hotel in the city of Cleveland. And the hotel itself has been the site of an amazing string of history. After Mowrey completed his simple tavern, the ghosts of Cleveland's past would march right by this sacred plot into history, mostly forgotten but fascinating nonetheless. Here are some snippets of history that occurred at the Hotel Cleveland and its predecessor hotels.

One of the first mass transit models in America was built in Cleveland. The Cleveland & Newburgh Railroad Company was incorporated on March 3, 1834, with capital of $50,000. Cleveland's first street railway built by Ahaz Merchant ran from Blue Stone Quarries in Newburgh township through orchards and woods to past Kennard Street. Then at Kennard Street (East Fifty-fifth Street and Carnegie Avenue), it completed its final trip to the southwest corner of Public Square, disappearing in the barn near the back of the Cleveland House (site of the current Hotel Cleveland). Two horses pulled a flat car on wooden rails, and at first only stone and lumber were hauled. Conveniences were added for passengers the next year, and Silas Merchant, driver, conductor, superintendent and barn man, made two trips daily.[57]

Perry's Victory Day—a once large celebration in Ohio that gave remembrance to Commodore Perry's victory over the British at the Battle of Lake Erie—on September 10, 1860, marked the opening of the Hower & Higbee store in a two-story building on Superior Street west of the square. This was the beginning of Cleveland's first department store, founded by Edward C. Higbee and John G. Hower, with five employees. Ten years later, it moved across the street (built on the current Hotel Cleveland site) into larger quarters. In 1897, Hower died, and Higbee became president. The firm name changed to the Higbee Company some five years later.[58] This is an important development for the Hotel Cleveland, for when it was originally built, the hotel was free standing, although a planned part of the more impressive Terminal Tower Complex by the Van Sweringen brothers. The hotel was counterbalanced, to a degree, by the Higbee Building along its eastern flank along Ontario Street. The Van Sweringens purchased the Higbee Company as part of the vast business empire and built a state-of-the-art department store as part of the Terminal Tower Complex.

And finally, one of the more dramatic moments in the hotel's history occurred when America's famed airman Charles A. Lindbergh was given an enthusiastic banquet reception at the Hotel Cleveland on August 1, 1927. At the event, Lindbergh declared, "It will be no more than three or four years before planes will be built for regular ocean service. They will mean faster communication between the nations. They will make for peace."[59] While his optimism for aviation as a tool for peace was shattered by the looming Depression and world war, his speech was well received.

A Serial Killer and Eliot Ness

Eliot Ness and his wife, Evaline, were frequent guests at the Hotel Cleveland's Bronze Room, a dance room with bronze-tiled walls and a walnut bar where big bands played every night of the week. Ness felt comfortable there, mingling with high-society figures and his fellow newsmakers. He could relax and let his guard down, but only halfway. Wherever he was, Ness always sat with his back to a wall, making sure to face the door.[60] As Cleveland's director of safety, Ness was responsible for the police and fire forces of the city, a position he took seriously.

Ness could count on the hotel's discretion for the more sensitive elements of his job. One of the macabre events of the Ness tenure in Cleveland was the torso murders. It was a captivating yet frightening period of time for the city as Ness and his vaunted police force struggled to solve a continuing saga of bloody murders in and around Kingsbury Run.

Kingsbury Run refers to an area along the east side of Cleveland near Shaker Heights that stretched westward through Kinsman Avenue and down to the Cuyahoga River. It also included a natural watershed that runs through East Seventy-ninth Street in Cleveland, where natural creeks drain storm water into the Cuyahoga River from areas that are now known as Warrensville Heights and Maple Heights. The name Kingsbury Run comes from James Kingsbury, the first inhabitant of Newburgh (1797) and one of the earliest settlers of the Western Reserve area. In the late 1800s, the city commissioned a new sewer tunnel system project through Kingsbury.[61]

The genteel nature of Kingsbury Run was lost on the residents of Cleveland from 1934 to 1938 when thirteen grisly murders were discovered within this area. The investigation had frustrated Ness, and the supposed serial killer was so emboldened that in 1936, he left the beheaded body of a tattooed young man near a police station located on East Fifty-fifth Street. The head was found nearby under a bridge. The police were so aggravated at the lack of clues that Ness ordered the police department to create a "death mask" of the young man and had it displayed at the vastly popular Great Lakes Exposition. The mask was a well-received display at the exposition with long lines and much gossip. Unfortunately, the police received few clues.

One of the more tantalizing suspects of the torso murders was Dr. Francis Sweeney. The doctor was born and raised in Kingsbury Run, and when he graduated from medical school in St. Louis in 1928, he returned to Cleveland and was immediately hired by St. Alexis Hospital, also located near the infamous run. He was a mammoth of man, a pillar of society, married to a beautiful woman and seemed to have secured the American dream after growing up as a hardscrabble youth.

Unfortunately, his life began to unravel soon after joining St. Alexis. His heavy drinking, card playing and womanizing did not sit well with his wife, and a divorce was imminent. The divorce fed his out-of-control lifestyle, and soon thereafter, he lost his prized job at the hospital. Still, he opened a private practice and frequented the local bars with impunity. The doctor would write prescriptions for narcotics for himself and his friends. He was a man unhinged, and he was Ness's number one suspect.

By the summer of 1938, Cleveland was in near hysteria over the murders. And desperate for answers, Elliot Ness made a curious decision by essentially kidnapping Dr. Sweeney and incarcerating him in the Hotel Cleveland. It was at the hotel over a number of days that Ness and a few others interrogated the doctor. Ness had to navigate the suspect's examination cautiously since Dr. Sweeney's cousin was the powerful congressman Martin L. Sweeney. If the congressman ever found out about this unethical tomfoolery, Ness's career would be over. Ness, however, thought the risk far outweighed the political issues, of which there were many. Consequently, the questioning continued, and a number of lie detector sessions were taken. The results were always the same. Dr. Sweeney was lying. Ness truly believed he had found the murderer, but even he admitted most of the evidence was circumstantial.[62] After a week or so hiding out in the Hotel Cleveland, Ness released Sweeney.

Upon his release, Sweeney immediately checked himself into a military sanitarium near Sandusky, Ohio. And thus began the strange sunset of his years. From August 25, 1938, until his death in 1965, Sweeney went from one hospital to another, both state mental hospitals and veterans' hospitals, in various parts of the country. He was not a prisoner and could leave the hospital voluntarily for days if not months at a time.[63] Sweeney later in his life would send Ness cryptic, taunting postcards about the murders. A number of these postcards now find their home at the Western Reserve Historical Society. It should be noted that there were no additional Kingsbury Run murders after 1938.

IN THE AUGUST OF ITS YEARS

The Sheraton Hotel chain acquired the Hotel Cleveland in 1958, renaming the hotel the Sheraton-Cleveland. Sheraton invested heavily in the hotel, including a $5.8 million ballroom, as well as updating the facility and some of the bars and restaurants.[64] In 1961, the famed Bronze Room—Elliot Ness's favorite place to unwind and indulge in camaraderie and booze—was transformed into the Kon Tiki, a colorful restaurant offering homage to the Polynesian restaurant craze that was captivating America. Cleveland was the third location for the Kon Tiki in a partnership between restaurateur Steven Crane and the Sheraton Hotels. The first two were built in Montreal, Canada, and Portland, Oregon. The 230-seat Kon Tiki consisted of a series of "intimate areas" that included a "tepe" entrance, bridge, pools and waterfalls, Maori Long Hut and a Luau Garden. It was quite a spectacle for the more staid Hotel Cleveland.

Unfortunately, the hotel upgrades and ballroom expansion could do little to ward off the decline in Cleveland's downtown area and the fortunes of the hotel. Another management team—Stouffer Corp.—took a chance on the Hotel Cleveland in 1978 and refurbished and renamed the hotel yet again as Stouffer's Inn on the square. The hotel was hoping to leverage the opening of the new mall within Tower City as developed by Forest City Enterprises in 1989 and again changed its name to Stouffer-Tower City Plaza. The 1991 renovation tore out a drop ceiling that had been put into place during one of the past renovations and restored the lobby to its past glory. This renovation also added the lobby fountain and the amazing chandeliers, all of which added to the hotel's sophisticated past. The hotel was sold again in 1993 to Renaissance International and is now known as the Renaissance Cleveland. In 2004, the Hotel's Grand Ballroom, still the largest ballroom in Cleveland, and the adjacent Exhibition Hall were remodeled. The hotel counts a lot fewer rooms—currently 491 rooms and 50 suites—than in times past, but the hotel is still a proud building. It is a symbol of the great times in Cleveland's rich past, a memorial for all of us in Cleveland to remember the rich history we are blessed with.

Opening night celebration at the Hotel Cleveland, 1918. *Photo courtesy of the* Cleveland Press *Archives.*

Lavelle Pierce, manager of the Hotel Cleveland, receives a medal for twenty years of service at the hotel. *Photo courtesy of the* Cleveland Press *Archives.*

Above: The Hotel Cleveland before the Terminal Tower building was constructed. *Photo courtesy of the* Cleveland Press *Archives.*

Left: A view of the Hotel Cleveland from Superior Avenue and West Sixth Street. *Photo courtesy of the Cleveland Public Library.*

Opposite, top: The Hotel Cleveland under construction. *Photo courtesy of the Western Reserve Historical Society.*

Opposite, bottom: A majestic buffet at the Hotel Cleveland. *Photo courtesy of the Western Reserve Historical Society.*

SEE CLEVELAND FLOWER SHOW
WAITE AUTO LIVERY
TAXICABS

Opposite, top: Some of Cleveland's finest relax outside the Hotel Cleveland. *Photo courtesy of the Western Reserve Historical Society.*

Left: The proposed ballroom at the Hotel Cleveland. *Photo courtesy of the Western Reserve Historical Society.*

Above: A behind-the-scenes look at the Sheraton Cleveland Hotel. *Photo courtesy of the Western Reserve Historical Society.*

HOTEL WINTON

The enterprising real estate editor of the *(Cleveland) Leader*—and later for the *Plain Dealer*—J.G. Monnett had just received another scoop on Cleveland's booming downtown marketplace. Big-monied interests out of Chicago had purchased a plot of land on Prospect Avenue and were about to announce a new twelve-storied hotel property tentatively to be named the Hotel Free after the developer involved with the transaction—J.L. Free. Mr. Free was a well-known realty operator at the time who believed that the growing metropolis of Cleveland could use another "Statler type" hotel in its exploding downtown area. Built for nearly $2.5 million, the building was designed by architect Max Dunning of Chicago. General contractor for the Hotel Winton was the Wells Brothers Company. C.M. Snyder, former manager of the Radisson and the Hotel LaSalle in Chicago, was the first general manager.[65]

The Hotel Free, during its construction, was renamed after the Cleveland automotive magnate Alexander Winton. It was a curious choice of a name for the new hotel, but the marketing brains behind the development thought having the building named after one of Cleveland's most beloved entrepreneurs would communicate to the Cleveland masses how enterprising and strong the Hotel Winton was to be. The hotel was, and still is, located at 1012 Prospect Avenue.

The first two stories of the twelve-story structure were built of stone while the upper stories were made of Blackstone brick and white terra cotta. Of the original six hundred rooms, two hundred started at $1.50 a day, and the others cost between $2.00 and $5.00 a day. The hotel had a separate service building. A special amenity for the hotel guests was "washed air year round, and iced in the summer to insure [*sic*] proper ventilation and cooling of all dining rooms."[66]

One of the unique features of the hotel was a short staircase from the lobby to a sub-mezzanine level that could seat nine hundred individuals for various meals. This large room would later become the world-famous Rainbow Room, a subterranean mecca of grand entertainment and world-class cuisine. The hotel's main kitchen, barbershop and private dining rooms were located here, too. The lobby area was finished in white marble and held offices, a grill and bar and a coffee shop. Four retail shops were designed for the Prospect Avenue building frontage.

A stunning set of white marbled steps led up from the lobby to a mezzanine floor that opened up into a banquet and small convention hall that could seat one thousand persons. The mezzanine offered six private dining rooms, the general manager's and controller's offices and six lavish suites, including the presidential suite. The mezzanine had a large balcony as well that offered a view of the lobby from an additional eight private dining rooms for special guests. Each of the nine floors above serviced sixty-one rooms each with its own bath and clothes closet—amazing amenities for the time.

Who Was Alexander Winton?

One could count on a single hand the number of cities that were growing as fast as Cleveland was during the post–Civil War era. Perfectly situated central to the vast ore and mineral deposits of the upper Great Lakes and the massive factories and foundries of Detroit and Pittsburgh, not to mention being a major player in the railroad system, Cleveland was blessed with good fortune and great geography. More entrepreneurs were minted in Cleveland during this period than anywhere else in the world.

When Horace Greeley wrote, "Go west, young man, go west and grow up with the country" in a *New York Tribune* editorial on July 13, 1865—he might as well have been talking about moving west from the eastern seaboard to a fine, fine destination known as Cleveland, Ohio. The opportunities in Cleveland were vast and the fortunes large. No one personified this more—with the exception of John D. Rockefeller—than Alexander Winton. He was a pioneer in automotive and marine technology.[67] And his name is still attached to many local venues, including Winton Towers in Lakewood, Ohio. This modern condo structure was, in fact, built on the grounds of Winton's estate along the banks of Lake Erie.

Winton was born in Scotland on June 20, 1860, and was educated in the "common schools of Scotland." He was an eager and very intelligent young man, especially in engineering, and was hired by the Clyde Ship Yards in 1873. It was tough work, but the shipyards offered to Winton a chance to see engineering, on a vast scale and on a daily basis. The dream, however, was the dream of a million other immigrants, and that was to somehow get to the United States—the land of opportunity. In 1878, Winton safely made it to America. He initially resided in New York, where he took employment at Delameter Iron Works as a machinist. After a year at the ironworks, he served as an assistant engineer aboard a cargo ship navigating between New York and South American ports.

The life at sea, unfortunately, was not for Winton. He was about to be married, and he thought he would find his fortune and fame in Cleveland. His sister lived in Cleveland and was married to a young man named Thomas W. Henderson. His first job in Cleveland was as a superintendent at the Phoenix Iron Works—which was then working on the massive powerhouse for the East Cleveland Railroad on Cedar Avenue (the building still exists on Cedar Avenue along Thackeray Avenue and Ashland Road). In 1890, Winton partnered up with brother-in-law Henderson to form the Winton Bicycle Company.[68] And soon thereafter the company started operations. The bikes were an immediate hit due to his knack for engineering and design. Winton bikes were made of tubing, not iron pipes, which made the bikes much lighter and faster. The bikes were also painted in various bright enameled colors and were easy to identify while being ridden.

Winton was a tinkerer of all things mechanical his whole life and is considered to have developed the first motorcycle in 1895.[69] It was this invention that focused Winton on a new concept of vehicle that could move more than one person at a time. So in 1897, Winton, his business partner Henderson and another gentlemen named George H. Brown formed the Winton Motor Carriage Company. Using a portion of a factory owned by Brush Electric Company, Winton and a crew of sixteen factory workers began production of the Winton carriage. In June 1897, the first Winton motor carriage was complete. In an effort to get publicity for the new contraption, the company invited a number of reporters to come out and literally kick the tires on the new Winton carriage.

The *Plain Dealer* reporter invited to the event, Charles B. Shanks, could not come to terms with what Winton had actually created and asked what benefit the motorized carriage could offer to someone. Winton remarked that his new vehicle could make it to New York City in less than fifty hours. A trip that lasts fifty hours today would get you to the other side of the planet—if not farther—but to suggest in 1897 that one could just hop into this carriage and drive to the East Coast was mind boggling. And so, on May 22, 1899, the trip to New York began on Public Square. Before Winton left, the mayor of Cleveland at the time, John H. Farley, handed Winton a letter addressed to the mayor of New York (which was delivered). From the time he left the Sixth City to when he finished in front of the Astor House some forty-seven hours and forty-three minutes later, his every movement was captured by press wire. Winton was a man of his word; his car could make it to New York in less than fifty hours. It was also during this trip that Shanks first coined the term "automobile."[70] (Shanks was eventually hired by Winton to be the advertising manager of Winton Motors.)

Unfortunately, Winton did not receive a hero's welcome in New York. Once in the city, a large crowd of curious spectators surrounded him, many of whom were peppering him with questions and ridicule.[71] After a few hours of humiliation (although he did get to talk to the mayor of New York and was a press sensation), he drove the car to a railroad station, loaded the car onto a train bound for Cleveland and returned home.

In 1898, Winton Motor sold twenty-two cars. The first Winton sold was purchased by Robert Allison Cole, who appeared at the factory with $1,000 in his pocket to buy the car he saw in an advertisement. This car is now at the Smithsonian and was declared the first production automobile sold in the United States. It was also in 1898 that Henry Ford came to Cleveland to interview for an engineer's position at Winton Motor. Winton came away unimpressed by the young Ford and did not hire him. Soon, people were buying and driving their Winton carriages everywhere. In 1899 came another Winton first; he created the first U.S. mail truck for the Cleveland postmaster.[72] He opened the first auto dealer in the United States in Reading, Pennsylvania.

Sales were strong enough in 1902 for Winton to move out of the Brush factory floor to a new state-of-the-art facility on West 117th Street and Berea Road. The facility also had a wooden test track for the carriages that wrapped around the factory. The building still stands but is in disrepair. From 1905 to 1910, Winton was the head, and the brand, of the largest car manufacturer in America. In fact, the plant itself was billed as the largest and finest-equipped exclusive automobile factory in the world.

In 1902, Winton started to design and build his yellow brick mansion on his twelve-acre lakefront site on Lake Avenue near Nicholson Avenue. He called his new mansion Roseneath after a small town in his native Scotland. He sold the mansion in 1924 and moved to a smaller estate at 18102 Clifton Road in Lakewood's Clifton Park neighborhood. Today, his Lake Avenue property is part of the Winton Place, the Gold Coast condominium built in 1964.

The curious Winton had another pull on his attention and time: his love of sailing and boating on the Great Lakes. As a youth, he traveled the world on a steamship. As a budding millionaire, Winton often took solitude in his steam-motored yacht. He didn't like the design and the torque of the engines, so he decided he would build his own engines. And thus started Winton Gas Engine & Manufacturing Company in 1911. The Winton Gas Engine Company specialized in gas-powered engines for maritime use. And by 1917, Winton again broke new ground by building the first diesel engines for use in boats and ships.

However, while the rest of the country was enjoying new wealth and new fun after World War I, Winton's business interests began to stumble. Every Winton carriage was custom built, and the new Ford Company was showing the world how the car could be made using mass production principles. The Winton Motor Company soon went into receivership. However, at the company auction, Winton did acquire the entire engine company that would be renamed the Winton Engine Company. The company prospered, and in 1927, he sold Winton Engine Company to secure his own financial future. General Motors then bought the company in 1930 and changed its name to the Cleveland Diesel Division.

No doubt a titan of industry, Winton was a low-key figure otherwise. He loved his family; his son followed in his footsteps at Winton Engine. He loathed politics, took little interest in civic affairs and did not participate in the private clubs that were all the rage then. He was an avid Mason and proud of his Thirty-second-degree Masonic rating. And until his death, he was a picture of great health and vigor.

The great myth, however, of Alexander Winton was that he was involved with the Hotel Winton. He was not. There are no records to indicate that he was an investor in the development, much less approached to be so. He never was quoted as saying he was miffed or amused by having a hotel named after him. He did not attend the formal opening of the hotel, and nothing could be found to note that he had ever walked through the beautiful lobby, halls or the Rainbow Room of the flagship hotel that carried his name.

Chef Hector Boiardi

A can of Chef Boy-Ar-Dee is an iconic food item for nearly every boy and girl in the United States. It shocks many to know that the chef pictured on the can was, in fact, a real person. And during his lifetime, he was not only an amazing chef but also a keen capitalist. He was born Hector Boiardi in 1897 in a small town in Italy. He was the son of Joseph and Maria Maffi Boiardi. By the age of ten, Boiardi began cooking in Italy and was considered a bit of a culinary prodigy.

At the age of seventeen, Boiardi followed his brother Paolo to the United States and joined the staff at the Plaza Hotel, working his way up to chef. He was then hired away by the Greenbrier Hotel in Greenbrier, West Virginia. It was at the Greenbrier that he served President Wilson. And when he was just twenty years old, the young Italian chef came to Cleveland to be the head chef at the Hotel Winton. Soon his spaghetti dinners were the talk of the town, and many of the hotel's patrons began to inquire how they might be able to take this dinner home with them. The chef, while a dynamic cook, knew a bit about business, too, and soon had created a take-home bag that included his special marinara sauce (in milk bottles), cheese, bread and pasta.

By 1923, he was newly married and had opened up his first restaurant, Il Giardino d'Italia (the Garden of Italy), on the corner of East Ninth Street and Woodland Avenue. His Italian dinners were all the rage. Many of his guests would ask for his recipes (which were not forthcoming from the chef) and for samples to take home (which he sold in abundance). Boiardi began using a factory in 1928 to fulfill all the orders for his food. And in 1938, Boiardi moved the factory to Milton, Pennsylvania, to be closer to the tomatoes and mushrooms he used in his recipes. For his food products sold to the public, he began to use the name Chef Boy-Ar-Dee.

A popular eatery along Euclid Avenue was the popular Pierre's Italian restaurant, named for its founder Pierre Pieratoni. Following his death in 1945, Pierre's was taken over by Boiardi, who had been operating Chef Hector's at 823 Prospect Avenue since 1931. Boiardi then joined with Albert Caminati to operate both Chef Hector's and Pierre's. Chef Hector's and Pierre's were favorites of those with a hankering for Italian cuisine, and both establishments had a loyal clientele. Chef Hector's closed in 1967, Pierre's in early 1974.[73]

Boiardi sold his interest in Chef Boy-Ar-Dee Quality Foods to American Home Foods after World War II for $6 million. He remained a consultant with the company until 1978. Boiardi took the proceeds from the sale to

American Home Foods to acquire Milton Steel, which he sold for a large profit in 1951. He lived the American dream and, in the process, became a fixture on the American dinner table.

After a short illness, the good chef passed away at his home in Parma, Ohio. At the time of his death, it was believed he was worth nearly $60 million. He was buried at the All Souls Cemetery in Chardon, Ohio. Boiardi was an iconic Clevelander, restaurateur and industrialist. And for a brief period of time, his culinary wonders made the Winton Hotel the must-attend place for Cleveland foodies. It was at the Winton Hotel where Boiardi honed the skills, both as a chef and a businessman, that served him so well for the rest of his life.

The World-Famous Rainbow Room

The Winton Hotel was quick to secure national fame for a number of reasons. Having a world-class and personable chef like Hector Boiardi certainly helped. But being the center of Cleveland nightlife also brought the Winton a lot of cache with ever-growing social circles of the Sixth City. The world-famous Rainbow Room was opened to great acclaim on December 16, 1932. It was a colorful and lively dining room capable of sitting nine hundred people for lunch or dinner.

One of the first radio programs to be broadcast nationally was produced out of the hotel's famous Rainbow Room and featured the Rainbow Room Orchestra. There were even "ice shows" at the Rainbow Room, where a large ice-skating rink was built near the orchestra section, and as patrons ate, there would be a number of ice skaters to entertain. National celebrities played in the dining room, and many conventioneers would brag to their cohorts that they got to see a show in the Rainbow Room.

The room itself was built below ground. When a patron or guest walked into the Winton Hotel lobby, a grand sign pointed them to stairs leading to the finest entertainment Cleveland had ever seen. Unfortunately, during the redevelopment of the hotel to low-rent apartments for the elderly, the Rainbow Room was destroyed so that the building could have a parking garage. It was a sad way for the grand room to end. But many residents swear that on a particularly quiet evening, one can hear the soft sounds of music emanating from the old Rainbow Room.

The Sweet Sounds of Artie Shaw

Artie Shaw was a prolific jazz composer and big bandleader and is widely regarded as one of jazz's finest clarinetists.[74] Born in New Haven, Connecticut, Artie Shaw arrived in Cleveland at the tender age of seventeen, hoping to launch his professional career. His first job in Cleveland was a musician in the Joe Cantor Band at the Far East Restaurant that used to be on Euclid Avenue.[75] A year later, Artie Shaw was gaining attention for his ability to arrange music and was offered a job with Austin Wylie and his Golden Pheasant Orchestra. Wylie was a jazz bandleader based in Cleveland, Ohio, but was on national radio broadcasts regularly.

Wylie and his Golden Pheasant Orchestra played eight hours a day at the Golden Pheasant Restaurant on Prospect Avenue next door to the Winton Hotel. Artie Shaw stayed at the Winton Hotel and roomed with another musician, Claude Thornhill. In 1929, Shaw wrote an essay and a musical composition entitled "Song of the Skies" for the National Air Races being held at the Cleveland airport. Shaw was becoming a national sensational and, in 1930, was offered a job with the nationally touring Irving Aaronson's Orchestra. With some hesitation, Shaw left the comforts of Cleveland. He occasionally would return, but his best days were ahead as his recording "Begin the Beguine" became world famous. He became an orchestra leader of his own and won the hearts of Lana Turner and Ava Gardner, among others. But for a brief period of time, the center of the jazz universe lived in a small, cramped room at the Winton Hotel.

The Albert Pick Company

At one time, the Albert Pick Company was the third-largest hotel chain in the United States. The company focused on large downtown hotels (unfortunately aging hotels) and an upscale level of service. Originally, the company was a hotel equipment house run by a gentleman named Albert Pick. The company also had a subsidiary that handled the organizing, financing and promoting of hotel operations. The Albert Pick Company was instrumental in the development, design and build of the Wade Park Manor Hotel, which opened in 1923, in University Circle. In 1926, Pick decided to create a new hotel company called the Pick Hotels Corporation.

The company's core hotels were old, grand hotels in urban areas that were going through tumult in the 1960s. And despite building eight profitable motels in the West to compete with the likes of Best Western and Holiday Inn, the company could not effectively compete with its new competition. Its Cleveland hotel, the Pick-Carter Hotel, was extensively renovated by the Albert Pick Company in the mid-1960s, but after a deadly fire, the company could not muster enough capital to rebuild the once grand and beautiful hotel despite its desire to do so. In the early 1970s, the Pick Hotels Corporation was sold to the Bass Brothers and combined with the Americana chain. The Pick-Carter Hotel in Cleveland was not included in the sale.

THE DEADLY FIRE

The Winton Hotel was sold to the Pick Hotel Chain, the fifteen-unit hotel chain created by Albert Pick out of Chicago, in the mid-1960s. In 1969, the now Carter-Pick Hotel went through a needed $1 million renovation plan. The renovation improved the lobby and lowered the room count but was considered a great upgrade. Business had started to improve for the hotel during this time.

It was a chilly spring day on April 14, 1971. The sun was shining, but the warmth was kept away as temperatures never reached forty degrees during the day. The thirteen-member cast of the national touring group for *Hair* and their families had checked into the hotel sometime during the afternoon. The cast joined another two hundred people with room reservations at the six-hundred-room hotel. It seemed to be a dynamic time with the lobby full of people during the day.

As night began to fall, the lobby emptied, and everything seemed well. The actors and cast of *Hair* were performing at a theater in Playhouse Square. It was just another quiet evening at the Pick Hotel. And then all hell broke lose. A wild conflagration ignited in the lower lobby ballroom and spread quickly throughout the hotel. Alarms were sounded, and people began to panic.

The Cleveland Fire Department made it to the hotel within minutes, but people were already hanging from third-, fourth- and fifth-floor windows, shouting for help.[76] Many hotel guests had to climb down fire ladders. Brave firefighters entered the flaming lobby of the hotel to lead others out of the inferno. It took 135 firefighters and nearly twenty fire trucks to calm the blaze.

The tragic fire had taken seven lives and nearly caused the deaths of a few firefighters, too. It left families in ruin. The stage manager of *Hair*,

Russell Carlson, lost his wife, Carroll, and his one-year-old daughter, Corina, in the fire. Cast member Jonathon Johnson also lost his wife, Robin, and daughter, Melissa, to the tragedy. It was the saddest day in the history of the Winton Hotel.

Not only did the fire take lives, but it also burned the will of the hotel itself. The Pick-Carter never reopened as a hotel despite the protestations of the Pick Hotel Chain. The building was eventually sold to a Cleveland enterprise and redeveloped as low-cost apartments.

The Short History of the Winton Hotel

In 1931, the hotel was taken over by the Metropolitan Life Insurance Company and renamed the Carter Hotel in honor of Lorenzo Carter, early pioneer, who built the first tavern in the village of Cleveland. Under its new name, the hotel and its famous Rainbow Room were formally dedicated on December 16, 1932, with a program including Governor George White, Mayor Ray T. Miller, Dr. Joel B. Hayden and orchestra leader Rudy Vallee with his Connecticut Yankees. Later, the Carter became a unit in the Albert Pick hotel system—renamed the Pick-Carter—with Allen Lowe as manager of the six-hundred-room establishment.[77]

After the deadly fire in 1971, the hotel lay dormant until 1972, when the William Passalacqua Builders Company acquired the building and decided to convert the hotel into a 280-unit apartment building. As part of the redevelopment of the now-defunct Pick Carter Hotel, the Federal Housing Administration approved a $5 million loan to aid in construction. The hotel was renamed again to the Carter Manor and focused on providing housing for the elderly. The financial model of the new Carter Manor never quite provided enough rents to pay off the highly leveraged facility, and in 1975, the U.S. Housing and Urban Development (HUD) department had to approve an emergency loan to keep the building from closing, thus putting on the streets a few hundred residents.

By 2009, the building—now called the Winton Manor—was focused on housing for the low-income elderly with 270 units. When inspected by HUD in 2009, the Winton Manor earned a Housing Quality Standards score of fifty-three out of one hundred, which means the living conditions of the property were significantly below the average of eight-six, which was considered healthy and safe by HUD. The rents, too, were nearly market rate with a one bedroom going for $920 a month, a decent sum for a Cleveland downtown rent in 2009. The building went through another renovation soon thereafter and was renamed, yet again, the Carter Manor.

The Winton Hotel never could match the history or the glamour of the Hotel Cleveland or Hotel Hollenden. The Hotel's Rainbow Room certainly gave the other hotels a run for their money. Nonetheless, the hotel is a grand building full of a wonderful history that all Clevelanders should cherish. The Hotel Winton certainly deserved better, but what a life it had!

A band plays for a large dinner party at the Hotel Winton. *Photo courtesy of the* Cleveland Press *Archives.*

The beautiful lobby of the Hotel Winton. *Photo courtesy of the* Cleveland Press *Archives.*

A large party being set up in the Rainbow Room. *Photo courtesy of the* Cleveland Press *Archives.*

Right: The Hotel Winton was renamed the Carter Hotel. *Photo courtesy of the* Cleveland Press *Archives.*

Below: Two of Hotel Winton's finest bartenders are ready to mix a few hearty libations. *Photo courtesy of the* Cleveland Press *Archives.*

The spectacular Carter Hotel. *Photo courtesy of the Cleveland Public Library.*

Tragedy strikes. A deadly fire at the Pick Carter Hotel. *Photo courtesy of the Cleveland Public Library.*

A distinguished mural near the ballroom of the Pick Carter Hotel. *Photo courtesy of the Cleveland Public Library.*

The famous Rainbow Room with a temporary ice rink at the Hotel Winton. *Photo courtesy of the Cardcow Images.*

LAKE SHORE HOTEL

Built along the leafy shores of Lakewood, Ohio, and nestled quietly in the Edgewater neighborhood is the Lake Shore Hotel. But don't let its quiet, beautiful façade fool you. The Lake Shore Hotel holds tight to its wonderful, rich history. When originally built in 1929, it was created to be the "Finest Residential Hotel between New York and Chicago." The Lake Shore Hotel opened at 12506 Edgewater Drive in Lakewood, located on a high bluff overlooking Lake Erie. A 450-room residential hotel of attractive architecture, it became the home of many executives associated with the industries of the Great Lakes region.[78] It is a building designed in a gorgeous Art Deco style.

County real estate records show the first entry on the land that is now the Lake Shore Hotel in 1860 as being part of Rockport, Ohio. William Smith owned the lot that was then part of the Plank Road with access to Lake Erie. By the 1880s, county records show the land being owned by a Catherine Dyer and used as access for two railroads—the New York City & St. Louis Railroad and the Rocky River Railroad. By the 1890s, the Rocky River Railroad no longer appeared on the real estate records. However, Rockport, Ohio, was now the Hamlet of Lakewood. Soon after, a street was cleared in front of the property called West Shore Drive (later to be called Edgewater Drive).

In 1920, Clyde and Mary Cummins purchased the land—which encompasses nearly four and a half acres—and called the wooded estate Oakcrest. In January 1928, Cummins announced plans to build the Lake Shore Hotel and selected Frank Bail as the architect. Bail designed the beautiful Fifth Church of Christ Scientist at West 117th Street and Lake Avenue, as well as the marvelous and majestic Cuyahoga County Juvenile Court building on East 22nd Street. Both buildings are unfortunately in serious states of disrepair.

The announcement of the Lake Shore Hotel was notable because it was the first hotel in Cleveland to take advantage of Lake Erie. Peabody & Company of Chicago completed the $3 million financing needed for the construction of the building. The original architectural plan for the building was to construct it in the form of a large U and to total 450 suites. Every room—singles or full suites—would have their own bathrooms. A large underground garage was constructed to house 180 cars. The Lake Shore Hotel was built ten stories high. Maid service was offered to all permanent tenants.

For the great convenience of guests, the hotel was to be connected to the lake by a graceful terrace leading to a "walled-in observation promenade." The building was constructed of steel frame and an exterior of Birmingham buff sandstone. The hotel was fireproof as well. Marine-styled flourishes were added to the interior for ornamentation. The main floor offered two dining rooms, which overlooked the lake, and a ballroom that could accommodate four hundred people. The first dining room was called the "Seaglade" and offered breakfast through dinner service. The atmosphere was more informal than the main dining room of the hotel. The carpet in the Seaglade was a deep orchid with little yellow lilies. A patron could dine in the mesmerizing room and then walk out onto a beautiful patio facing Lake Erie. The patio offered small chairs and tables for a late-night drink and had a tea service during the afternoons.

Attached to the lobby was the Octagon Room, a luscious, reserved area for guests to relax and wait for the formal dining room—"The Nautilus"—to open. Several beautiful paintings and a soft splashing fountain added a restful charm to the room.[79] The Nautilus served as the formal dining and social room of the Lake Shore Hotel overlooking the lake, patio and gardens.

The rooms at the Lake Shore were designed for the ultimate comfort of the resident. The full suites each had a large kitchen, but delivery from the dining room was available. Living rooms and bedrooms of the Lake Shore were much larger than most resident hotels—hence the reason so few suites were built relative to the Hotel Statler, which had one thousand rooms—giving the illusion of a luxurious private residence. A nursery was also offered to tenants for their children. The entire lobby and dining room areas were decorated in a nautical theme. As noted in the *Plain Dealer Magazine*:

> *In keeping with the hotel's location on a beautiful inland sea, the building was decorated with marine motifs. Pairs of fish and sea horses were carved*

> *in stone above the entrance. Copper sea horses climbed the edge of the scalloped copper canopy. Stone sea creatures clung to the roof. Lighted stone seashells ornamented the brick and sandstone walls.*
>
> *Inside the aquatic imagery continued in other forms. A swirling ceiling was shaped like a wave above the vestibule. Cast-iron sailfish supported the gates to the dining room. Plaster seagulls flew toward the ribbed ceiling… Indian chiefs glowed by the light of graceful Art Deco wall sconces.*[80]

It was a majestic building. There was nothing like it in Cleveland.

In 1929, the Lake Shore had planned to build a glass enclosure to its fabulous patio facing Lake Erie. The double French glass plates would have allowed residents, guests and transients to dance on the patio in winter as well as summer. Plans were also completed that year to build three piers on the lakeside of the hotel. The piers would have created a small harbor for small boats and provided access to a "bathing beach."[81]

Unfortunately, the hotel opened just as the Great Depression was beginning. In early 1929, the hotel was placed in receivership. Theodore De Witt, then manager of the Hotel Hollenden, was appointed operating receiver for the Lake Shore Hotel on January 3, 1929. Freer-Heene Company, a bonding enterprise with offices in the Union Trust Company building, filed the petition for receivership. The petition listed $150,000 owed to Hartman Wholesale Furniture and other bills totaling $100,000. In early 1932, the hotel finally made its way out of receivership and was placed in a new corporation controlled by Peabody & Company.

In 1934, the new owners launched a novel addition to the Cleveland nightlife by opening the Pent House Club on the tenth floor. The Pent House Club had a dramatic view of Lake Erie. What was once the large suite of a resident was, within weeks, turned into the hottest nightclub in Cleveland. Over two hundred guests crowded the former flat that was turned into a large ballroom. The nightly entertainment was John Can Dull's Orchestra. Every room in the club was a different color with various designs. A closet was turned into the orchestra stall. The former library now housed the "well-stocked" Colonial Bar.[82] A veranda was also created on the roof attached to the Pent House Club. A world-famous bartender, Johnnie Quigley, was hired away from Jimmy Walker, former mayor of New York City, to create exotic libations and cocktails. The club was a huge success.

The original promise of a pool was not realized at the Lake Shore until 1956, when the owners of the hotel built the Lake Shore Swimming Pool & Cabana. The private club, with a built in tiki bar, became the coveted invite by many each summer. The cost of building the pool and cabana was $200,000. The pool was an aquamarine-colored oasis next to the stone Art Deco hotel. Flanking the east side of the pool was the two-story cabana building, which provided a buffer between the swimmers and sunbathers. The pool also had two hundred lockers to its south. Umbrella areas were to the north with views of the lake and the famed tiki bar. The pool was closed forever in 1971. Sold to the developers of the Waterford condominium.

The hotel went through a modest renovation in late 1961. Nearly $70,000 was spent to clean the front entrance of the building and to create a larger parking lot in front of the building. A new restaurant built out in the lobby area was called the "Hunt Room" and was paneled in light oak. New chandeliers and drapes were also added to the Hunt Room.

A new owner took control of the Lake Shore Hotel in the spring of 1964. Frank P. Celeste, former mayor of Lakewood, acquired the building for $1 million. Celeste was the president of Shore Hotel Towers, Inc. He was quite instrumental in building the Gold Coast in Lakewood, a group of famous condo towers that hug the Lake Erie coastline just to the west of the Lake Shore.

In 1971, it was announced that a $1 million renovation would take place and turn the suites in the hotel into low-rent apartments for senior citizens. A Federal Housing Authority loan was secured for the project. A nearby building—the Westerly Apartments—was also turned into a senior living facility. It was then renamed the Lake Shore Towers. By the end of 1985, the Lake Shore was acquired by Showe Management Company out of Columbus, Ohio. Also during 1985, the final public restaurant at the hotel, now called the Marius Restaurant, closed. Soon thereafter, the eastern part of the lobby and restaurant was taken over by Lakewood-based architect Jim Larsen and his architectural firm, Larsen & Associates. The company still occupies this gorgeous space today.

THE COMINGS AND GOINGS AT THE LAKE SHORE HOTEL

The Lake Shore Hotel was robbed by a masked gunman wearing overalls on the evening of October 6, 1929. His dress marked him as the fellow who had robbed eighty people at a Detroit Avenue tearoom the week before. Somehow, he had entered the cashier's room through a side door, held up three hotel workers and "ransacked" the hotel for the rich sum of $32.[83]

During the hold-up, a female clerk of the hotel unknowingly knocked over an envelope from her desk; it held $698 in cash. The "overall robber" never noticed. Nothing was ever heard of the robber again.

In 1937, a general hotel strike was called by the powerful unions in Cleveland. The Hotel Service Employees Union called the strike because the management of the Lake Shore refused to recognize the union. The strike affected both the Lake Shore and the Hotel Westlake in Rocky River. Of the ninety-seven hotel employees, only fifteen were union workers. But none passed the picket line. However, guests and tenants were allowed to send out their housekeepers and chauffeurs for groceries and supplies. To make matters worse, the heat and hot water were shut off during the dispute.

Sitting atop the grand hotel was a twenty-foot-high brilliantly lit sign spelling out "Lake Shore." The sign extended eighty-feet along the roof of the hotel. Many ships sailing on the Great Lake could see the letters from miles away and immediately knew their proximity to the docks of the Cleveland port. It was installed in 1930 by Fred Irwin, a resident of the hotel who pioneered neon signs.[84] The sign was seen as a part of the neighborhood. Unfortunately, as the towering condo buildings along the Gold Coast were built, many of the new neighbors complained. It seems the night on the Gold Coast was as bright as day when the large neon sign was turned on. The complaints had reached a fever pitch in 1964, and it was decided the sign would be turned off and torn down. The sign was missed.

The seventieth-anniversary celebration for the now Lake Shore Towers was held on August 7, 1999. The mayor of Lakewood at the time, Madeline Cain, joined Congressman Dennis Kucinich and many other guests to reminisce about the grand hotel. The guests enjoyed the music of Vincent Delcalzo, who was a member of the WPA Opera Company during the Great Depression, and the pianist Don Kimble. It was a beautiful, sunny day with temperatures in the mid-eighties—a perfect day to celebrate the Lake Shore Hotel's longevity.

Final Thoughts on the Lake Shore Hotel

The Lake Shore Hotel was the first of thirteen residential high-rises along the Gold Coast in Lakewood, Ohio. The "Coast" is only three-quarters of a mile long yet comprises more than 2,800 various suites and over 3,200 tenants and represents $60 million in construction costs. But no other building along the Gold Coast can compare to the beauty of the fine Lake Shore Hotel. It was home to many notable individuals, including Dr. C.L. Graber, founder of Lakewood Hospital. Many celebrities found the Lake Shore Hotel a luxurious place to call home, albeit temporarily. Famed swimmer Eleanor Holm, actresses Jean Harlow and Carol Channing and actor Dick Powell all stayed at the Lake Shore. There are rumors that Al Capone once found restful sleep at the Art Deco masterpiece. The hotel was so swank that Mike Douglas called it home when he was given his famous Cleveland talk show.

It was a beauty. And it still is. The hotel stands as a testament to great design. A stunning example of grand architecture, hotel stands prominently on Edgewater Avenue, a vanguard to the newer towers along the Gold Coast. But don't let age deceive you with the Lake Shore. The hotel will remain while all the other condos near it disappear. The Lake Shore is a visually stunning feast of architecture and a keeper of a glorious past.

The grand sign of the Lake Shore Hotel. *Photo courtesy of the* Cleveland Press *Archives.*

The swimming pool and cabana area of the Lake Shore Hotel. *Photo courtesy of the* Cleveland Press *Archives.*

A view from Lake Erie up to the Lake Shore Hotel. *Photo courtesy of the* Cleveland Press *Archives.*

The back porch area of the Lake Shore Hotel. *Photo courtesy of the* Cleveland Press *Archives.*

The dining room area of the Lake Shore Hotel. *Photo courtesy of the* Cleveland Press *Archives.*

The impressive Lake Shore Hotel. *Photo courtesy of the Cleveland Public Library.*

A remarkable aerial view of the Lake Shore Hotel. *Photo courtesy of the Cleveland Public Library.*

The Lake Shore Hotel offered a beautiful dining room for guests. *Photo courtesy of the Cleveland Public Library.*

Architectural renderings of the pool and cabana area of the Lake Shore Hotel. *Photo courtesy of the Cleveland Public Library.*

The beautiful design of the Lake Shore Hotel. *Photo courtesy of the Cleveland Public Library.*

HOTEL STATLER

The formal opening of Hotel Statler at the northwest corner of Euclid Avenue and East Twelfth Street made October 19, 1912, a memorable date. There were two great banquets on the mezzanine floor, one of which was given in honor of E.M. Statler by eastern hotel executives and the other by Charles L. Pack for many of his business associates. Elaborate entertainment was planned for the public opening, and fine orchestras played for the assembled crowds. The seven-hundred-room building was modern and complete, one of the nation's finest hostelries. Its beautiful ballroom became the meeting place of business and social organizations and the scene of many brilliant events. The first manager was James P.A. O'Connor, who was succeeded by T.P. Cagwin.[85] The property, fronting 104 feet on Euclid Avenue, was purchased by Pack for $150,000. In 1911, it was leased to the Hotel Statlers Company at a maximum rental of $34,000 a year on a valuation of $750,000.[86]

The seven-hundred-room hotel was designed by George B. Post & Sons with Charles Schneider, who would later make his own reputation as a residential architect, as supervisor. According to his biographer, Post was "one of those responsible for the development of the typical modern hotel plan, with its hundreds of rooms, each with a bath, and a monumental suite of public rooms below—all arranged to give the maximum income through the leasing of shops and concessions. Following Post's death in 1913, his sons designed a number of other Hotel Statlers in other cities."[87]

The Statler reeked of sophistication. There was little doubt among Statler executives that the Cleveland hotel was the chain's crown jewel. It was considered the most elegant hotel in the Statler chain, and it prided itself on the Statler philosophy that "the guest is always right." By 1920, the Hotel Statler had added an additional three hundred rooms, building an extension on the original hotel west along Euclid Avenue. The ground, first and second floors were held by the Stillman Company, which then operated the Stillman Theater out of the facility. This expansion cost the Statler family nearly $300,000 to finish.

The hotel was instrumental in local radio history as well. WGAR, a five-hundred-watt radio station, opened in the Hotel Statler on December 15, 1930, under the direction of John F. Patt, vice-president and general manager. It had nineteen employees and was affiliated with the National Broadcasting Company–Blue Network. Two years later, the station was using one thousand watts in the daytime and five hundred at night. Before its first decade was concluded, a new antenna tower was constructed, a mobile unit was equipped and complete offices were opened. In 1937, WGAR became a unit in the Columbia Broadcasting chain. It adopted the slogan "Cleveland's Friendly Station" and proved its friendliness by airing many programs advancing the interests of the city.[88]

The hotel found itself a victim of a union strike in 1935. Management of the hotel and the American Federation of Labor could not agree on fair wages and other labor demands. The Statler was marked by vandalism and stench bombings. It seems on October 28, 1935, a stench bomb was hurled into a conduit chute, stinking up the mezzanine of the hotel. Guests were not amused.

In 1938, the hotel announced a $500,000 upgrade to its rooms. The upgrades included new bright-colored draperies, carpets, bed coverings and "innerspring mattresses." New ceiling fixtures replaced the small chandeliers in each room. A wall panel at the room entrance, a truly novel invention at the time, now controlled lighting.

Conrad Hilton and his famous Hilton chain were looking to make a splash in the Cleveland market. And in 1954, Hilton acquired the famed Hotel Statler. In fact, Hilton purchased the entire Statler chain for $111 million in what was then the world's largest real estate transaction.[89]

At the time, the Cleveland Hilton Hotel Statler was considered one of the finest properties in the large Hilton chain. But the building was beginning to show its age, and despite a $3.5 million investment into the hotel in 1965, the Statler could not increase its occupancy rates enough to keep it in the Hilton family. The Hilton Company sold the Statler to a group of New York investors headed by Otto Marx, an investment banker, for nearly $2 million in August 1965. Marx was the president of the Paribas Corp., which is now part of BNP

Paribas Investment Banking. The Hilton Company was retained to manage the facility. The hotel announced in October 1965 that a new remodeling would take place. A $2 million investment was focused on a dramatic expansion of its ballroom. The remodeled ballroom would be expanded to accommodate 1,500 people for dinner and nearly 2,200 for a meeting. The 1965 remodeling would double the ballroom, which had not changed since the hotel was built in 1912.

Additional remodeling in 1965 included a new Mayflower Coffee Shop, a new La Cantina cocktail lounge (on the site of the old Terrace Room), a new escalator from the lobby to the ballroom floor and a complete renovation of 500 of the then 882 rooms. The Hilton Company, prior to the sale to Paribas, also authorized the remodeling of the hotel's famous Café Rouge. Three airline offices were added to the lobby as well. It was also during the 1965 remodeling that the new parking garage, site of the former Stillman Theater, was connected to the lobby.

The new owners—Paribas Corporation—converted several floors of the hotel to office space in 1971 to make the building more profitable. The name of the Statler was changed to the Cleveland Plaza in 1973. But the building continued to spiral down in terms of room and office occupancy. A local group of investors headed by Carl Milstein purchased the building in 1981 for $1.5 million. Milstein was a well-known developer in northeast Ohio who had literally built Brookpark, a suburb near Cleveland, in the 1950s. Soon thereafter, he became the largest builder of subsidized building complexes in northeast Ohio. He is perhaps best known today as the once proud owner of Northfield Park racetrack. In any case, Milstein made the decision to shutter the hotel and turn the entire building into an office complex. As part of the redevelopment, he brought in the Swingos brothers—Jim and Nick—to build a Swingos restaurant at street level on East Twelfth Street. Milstein named the building the Statler Office Tower. The building suffered many years as a Class C office space until 2001, when the building was converted into 295-apartment unit. The name changed again to the Statler Arms. The once stunning hotel now thrives as a downtown residence.

La Cosa Nostra

It was a cold, blustery night along East Twelfth Street. The winds from Lake Erie were doing a number on the city. Patrolman Frank Osowski was working his patrol up East Twelfth onto Euclid Avenue. It was four thirty in the morning on December 5, 1928. Patrolman Osowski was wet, frozen and praying to get around the block one more time before he would make his way to the police station on Payne Avenue. Two well-polished touring cars sped past him as he walked south toward Euclid Avenue. At first, the police officer didn't take much stock in the moment. He just wanted to find some warmth. But as he passed the passengers of the cars, now emptying out and making their way into the lobby of the grand Hotel Statler, he thought something was a bit suspicious.

After a few minutes of standing outside in the cold, Patrolman Osowski walked into the lobby noticing a few of the well-dressed men loitering around the lobby, smoking, not talking a lot, ignoring the patrolman. In less than a half hour, all the men had checked in, registered and made their way to their rooms. The cars were valeted, and the hotel lobby returned to an early morning quiet before the rush of breakfast patrons. Osowksi, noting none of the newly arrived guests were around, walked to the hotel counter and asked to see the registry. While there were only eleven men who arrived by the two sedans, he noticed a total of twenty-three out-of-town guests with exotic last names.

Osowski hastily made his way back to the station and informed the on-duty officer, Lieutenant Kurt Gloeckner, of what he had witnessed at the stately Hotel Statler. It was about 10:00 a.m. on the morning of December 6 when the lieutenant and a handful of plainclothes detectives made their way into the lobby of the Hotel Statler. Gloeckner and the hotel manager conferred about the guests. Could the guests have been in town for a wedding? A funeral? Were they businessmen and this was just a misunderstanding?

The lieutenant used the lobby telephone to call for additional patrolmen and a couple of paddy wagons, noting that they should park the vehicles behind the hotel off East Twelfth Street. One of the porters told Gloeckner that all of the men were in a meeting parlor. The lieutenant was sweating at the temples hoping he was not making a colossal mistake that could impugn his solid career. He gave the order, and the policeman quickly filed into the parlor arresting the twenty-three mysterious guests. Quietly, all of the men were taken down a freight elevator into the alley, placed into paddy wagons and taken to the Payne Avenue police station.

As Lieutenant Gloeckner and a few other plainclothes officers walked onto Euclid Avenue, there were big smiles and quick congratulations. But even then, how could they know that Cleveland's finest had just raided the first ever meeting of La Cosa Nostra?

By December 7, the mysterious guests were in court for a bond hearing. City manager W. Hopkins (Cleveland Hopkins Airport is named after him) found no friends in the police department by questioning the tactics used in the arrests. All of the arrested men were of "foreign-birth or parentage." Some did not speak any English. The gangsters were freed on $10,000 bond each (and all made bail supplied by local "friends") but were forced to stay in Cleveland for one week while city attorneys reviewed the property pledged on the bonds. The city attorneys quickly discovered the items pledged on the bonds were not of significant value or did not exist.

But it was the capture of one Clevelander during this mêlée that cemented the thought of mob involvement. The man was Sam Pallacco, a lieutenant in the local mob, known in the press as the "sugar baron of the rum trade." Pallacco had worked for "Big Joe" and John Lonardos before they were slain by a rival gang. The brains behind the meeting of the high dons of the mafia were Joe Porrello and Sam Tilocco. The Cleveland police picked up some incredible names, legendary in the history of the American mob, during the Statler raid, including Joe Profaci, founder of the Colombo mafia family. Vincent Mangano, founder of the Gambino family, was another victim of the accidental police sting.[90] Eventually, the men were released and went their separate ways. The history of the mob in Cleveland runs deep. And it is a fascinating history, which makes it all the more amazing that it's widely acknowledged that the first ever meeting of La Cosa Nostra was, in fact, to have taken place in Cleveland at the Hotel Statler.

THE ARCHITECTURE OF THE HOTEL STATLER

The hotel was built in an English Renaissance style called the Adams period. While many architects considered the Statler built along Italian lines, great care had been extended by the hotel owners to maintain the Adams characteristics in the minutest details. The Adams brothers—Robert and James—who fathered the style abundantly on display at the Statler, lived and worked in the eighteenth century. The brothers trained under many Italian masters.

Marble halls and the use of blue and gold in the lobby were to overwhelm and inspire the hotel guests. The lobby was enormous—104 feet wide and 329 feet long. The walls and pillars were of Botticini marble; the ceiling was of plaster relief with panels of ivory and blue. The ceiling was described by the *Plain Dealer* at the time as "one of the finest ceilings in the world." Throughout the lobby were bold divans with small semicircular tables.

There were writing tables and "easy chairs" also scattered throughout the lobby. The furniture was Italian walnut covered in blue silk brocade, and all the tables, desks, divans and chairs were inlaid with beautiful blue medallions. Chinese rugs were spread throughout the lobby, as well. There were handsome walnut reading lamps with blue and gold silk shades.

The Statler's formal dining room was conveniently off the large lobby and was decidedly Italian in its style. The room was decked out in ivory and rose colors. Two electrically lighted fountains with tiny bronze figures played soft, enchanting music from marble niches on either side of the dining room. It was a stunning room. The room itself was called the "Clevelander" and was considered by hotel management (outside of the Pompeian Room) as the social center of the hotel. Nine murals decorated by William Welch, a young Cleveland artist, were painted throughout the room. The murals depicted various eras in the hospitality industry. Another Cleveland artist, Miss Grace Walsh, created a number of tiny panels for the dining room representing classical figures in history.

Adjoining both the lobby and the dining room was the Pompeian Room. It was a showcase of a room that became nationally famous for its gorgeous accommodations and world-class service. Huge Pompeian pillars rose up to a series of balconies decorated with fern boxes and topped by extended rafters and trellises, from which hung large nasturtiums, a vibrant type of flower. The ceiling was painted a Pompeian blue and highlighted a wonderful skylight. The room was finished with antique wood effects, with Pompeian red and "Caen stone" as the prominent colors. The tables had small bronze lights with orange-colored silk shades that cast a strange glow over the tables. The *Plain Dealer* noted at the opening of the hotel: "It is a most decided contrast to the rest of the hotel, but to those who have a taste for the bizarre, the Pompeian will be the favorite dining room."

A billiard room was comfortably found off the lobby area. It was built in a Tyrolese style with paneled oak and beamed ceilings and the customary old red leather furnishings. The hotel also offered a large barbershop designed entirely in white. The shop offered fifteen chairs of white enamel with each barber having his own sanitizing equipment. For the hotel's female guests, the barbershop had a manicure department with white enameled tables that included inset bowls and faucets of hot and cold water.

Above the lobby, billiards rooms and bar area was the "society floor," or mezzanine floor. The floor was brilliant and decorated in blue and gold to harmonize with the floor below. The ballroom was immediately off the mezzanine section. The ballroom was painted and decorated in red and gold with numerous private dining areas surrounding the room. The main private dining room was the "lattice room" and had a French inspiration. The room's walls were latticed with little cameos interspersed on walls and ceiling and with a unique set of Wedgewood cameo doorknobs. The room's draperies were soft green-and-yellow striped silk.

The barroom and grill were distinctively English in style, emphasizing heavy oaken panels, beamed ceilings and leaded-glass windows. The furnishings were antique, the chairs a red leather and the floor a dull green tile with iron fixtures. Over the bar was a paneled painting of "grotesque figures, gnomes and elves." A large fireplace completed the informal air of the bar. At the back of the barroom and grill was a sizeable library many called the Mecca with yet another large fireplace and walls with built-in oak bookcases containing hundreds of volumes of lore. The hotel even went so far as to hire an expert librarian to manage the room. There was an elevated portion of the Mecca that was equipped with desks and writing materials. And for those who didn't want to expend energy writing their own letters, there was a public stenographer on staff for the guests' use.

The parlor floor was located on the third floor, which consisted of a number of small parlors. The parlors were decorated in various colors, including blue, green, lavender, ivory and gray. The furniture in the well-appointed parlors were Chippendale in style in mahogany and walnut.

All floors above the parlor floor consisted of the seven hundred sleeping rooms (later expanded to one thousand). Every room in the Hotel Statler had a private bath, including a shower—a welcomed upgrade to most hotels at the time. Every room had a desk phone that rang to the hotel operator to connect with an outside line. All rooms had a portable bronze lamp, and some had closets. Those that did not have a closet had a dresser with glass doors. A unique innovation of the Hotel Statler was lights built into each dresser. The paintings or art in the rooms were generally a Reynolds, Gainborough, Landseer or Van Dyke. On top of every dresser was a pincushion furnished with needles and thread for any modest tailoring needs of the patron.

One of the more unique innovations found at the Hotel Statler was a "contrivance" on the doors of each room that alerted the maid staff that someone had either entered or left the room. Additionally, ice water was piped into each bathroom. The bathrooms, too, had a unique system of levers, which controlled the temperature and level of the water for a bath or shower.

The Hotel Statler was an architectural and engineering marvel and was deservedly considered a high-end hotel in Cleveland. Its rich history should highlight the importance of this hotel to the then rapidly growing Sixth City. The Hotel Statler in Cleveland literally propelled the chain into a national powerhouse and gave importance to the man who started it all.

The Man Behind the Hotel Statler

E.M. Statler had single-handedly built the Hotel Statler chain. His first hotel was built in Buffalo, New York, in 1901 for the Pan-American Exposition. Despite the fact that the exposition was a failure (primarily due to the assassination of President McKinley), Statler learned a great deal on how to create a great experience for the hotel guest. The Pan-American Hotel was a temporary structure. His first permanent hotel was also built in Buffalo in 1907. It was a huge success. The opening-night price for a room was $1.50 per guest, leading to the famous Hotel Statler slogan: "A room and a bath for a Dollar and a Half." Statler made a unique observation about Americans around the turn of the century. He noticed that the prosperous country had produced a large, mobile group of travelers. And his hotels focused on this niche for many, many years.

In 1912, he built the magnificent Hotel Statler in Cleveland. Others followed in Detroit, St. Louis and New York. Statler was famous for his various "maxims" on service, prices and tips. He firmly believed that the guest is always right. He studied what prices to charge on everything from rooms to food. He felt it was important to study the character of his employees. And he wanted to create a universal experience in his hotels. Walking into the Hotel Statler in Cleveland would be as familiar an experience as walking into the Detroit Hotel Statler. His most famous maxim was: "A hotel has just one thing to sell, and that is service."[91] Statler's famed "Service Code" was to be found in every room. The code dispensed ideas and service guidelines for employees and guests alike. The code included topics from tipping ("Please do not tip unless you feel like it. But if you do tip, let your tipping be yielding to a genuine desire—not conforming to an outrageous custom") to hiring good-natured people ("Get rid of the grouches"). And the service of a Hotel Statler was well received and expected to be extraordinary. Statler died in 1928 before his chain would hit its pinnacle when purchased by Hilton Hotels in 1954.

Once the leading chain for business travelers across the United States, the Statler name is faded and nearly forgotten (although one of the curmudgeons of Muppets fame is named Statler and the other Waldorf—both named after the famed hotel chain founders).[92] But for a brief period of time, the Statler name was gold. His hotels were the envy of other hoteliers. The Statler would become a national chain with hotels built from coast to coast. Unfortunately, few of the original Statler buildings have survived.

The World-Famous Terrace Room

To the delight of many theatergoers in Playhouse Square, the Statler remodeled and opened its famous Terrace Room and Lounge Bar in late 1937. It was a sold-out affair as many in the crowd enjoyed "a quick bracer" before dinner. Famous pianist Roger Stearns played to the four hundred happy patrons, although he "struggled against the odds of an entirely inadequate piano."[93]

The Terrace Room occupied the space that was once the gorgeous Pompeian Room. The space offered an elliptical and sunken dance floor that was a striking feature for the room. The ceiling above the room was "cave-shaped and tricky lights fill the cave with gorgeous blue and red and misty shades."[94] Circling the dance floor, in a sort of balcony effect, were the tables. The Terrace Room had an eclectic color scheme of peacock blue, white and light red with all the metalwork in gold. The orchestra would sit at the north end of the room and would play in front of a screen that displayed murals of tigers and fawns.

The new Lounge Bar took over a number of shops on Euclid Avenue and had its own street entrance. To say it was one of the most magnificent bars in Cleveland history would be a great understatement. The walls of the bar were completed in Japanese ash wood. Behind the bar was another mural that showed a group of Greeks enjoying themselves in the pleasures of drinking, music and dancing, and in the foreground is a fawn whose startled eyes gaze directly into the room.[95] The ceiling of the lounge was covered in gold leaf and had concealed lighting.

Walker & Weeks, a famous Cleveland architectural firm, conceived the impressive and swank Terrace Room and the Lounge Bar. Emerson Construction finished the manufacture of the two beautiful rooms. Rudolf Bundas and Paul Riba painted the murals in the two rooms. Rudolph Bundas, a resident of Seattle, was a commercial artist who also painted portraits and landscapes in watercolor and oil. He studied at the Cleveland Art Institute, Western Reserve University and on art fellowships in Europe. Riba was born in Ohio and received his professional training at the Pennsylvania Academy of the Fine Arts. He graduated with highest honors from the Cleveland Institute of Art, where he taught for fourteen years.

Both the Lounge Bar and the Terrace Room were gorgeous and fulfilled the entertainment desires of numerous Clevelanders for years. However, by the early 1960s, both were used infrequently. Winsor French, a famous society columnist for the *Cleveland Press*, castigated the Hotel Statler during this period for closing his "field office" in what reads like an obituary for the intimate nightlife Winsor once treasured:

> *The other afternoon…I looked into the old bar where Roger Stearns used to serve as host, struck a few matches and found the place exactly as it always was. The little piano is still there, the tables are stacked neatly in a corner and the giddy murals still stare down from the shadowed walls—none the worse for the passing years. It would be nice if the Statler would suddenly remember this was the most attractive and successful cocktail lounge in town and open it again.*[96]

JUST ANOTHER HOTEL STATLER CRIMINAL STORY

One would think that after a national story of Cleveland police arresting high-ranking mob bosses from across the country that criminals might want to stay away from the Hotel Statler. Yet that was not the case. In 1937, the grand hotel was the scene of another twisted, illogical story of a hoodlum trying to hide in plain sight.

A young man by the name of Bob Murray somehow found a job as a busboy in one of the Hotel Statler's dining rooms. He was affable, quiet, had a penchant for white soap carving (a national phenomena at the time) and was a pretty good sketch artist. Unknown to others at the hotel, he was also a con artist and murderer.[97] Murray was always timely and, during the down times of his shift, gave a lot of attention to a young lady named Henrietta Koscianski. She was a pantry maid at the hotel and was taken aback by the busboy's looks and his worldly ways. Henrietta could never quite shake the fact that he seemed to be more than just a busboy.

One night at the hotel when business was slow, Murray approached the statuesque Koscianski to sit for him while he sketched her in the empty dining room. Murray was quick with the pencil and was rather skilled. Koscianski mentioned how she enjoyed being drawn, and he asked if he could keep the sketch. She agreed. Now finished with sitting for the busboy, she made her way to an employee lounge to gossip with a friend. Koscianski's friend also happened to have a number of newly published detective magazines.

As Koscianski and her friend chatted, she was glancing through one of the detective magazines when she stopped cold. A black-and-white photograph had caught her eye and sent the proverbial shivers up her spine. The man in the photo was an identical match to Bob Murray! The photograph was part of a story on a man named Robert Irwin—a fugitive in a triple murder and wanted by the New York City police.[98]

She could not believe that the kind artist laboring as a busboy was in fact a coldblooded murderer. Koscianski, two days after reading the magazine, started to tease Murray, calling him the "murderer." He seemed good-natured about it and denied ever knowing a Robert Irwin. But something just wasn't right, and Koscianski finally decided to play it safe and called the police. When the police arrived, they found that Murray had taken flight. It seems life on the run was starting to catch up to Murray, and he knew it. Soon after, when Murray had made his way to Chicago, he called one of the Chicago newspapers, giving them an exclusive on the murder. He was arrested in Chicago and was sent back to New York for trial.

The Comings and Goings of the Hotel Statler

The Hotel Statler lived a full life. And the hotel always seemed to be in the news. It offered the thriving Sixth City a valuable venue for intrigue, high society, crime and salacious stories. That's what makes the Statler one of the more fascinating hotels to have operated in Cleveland. The following clips were taken from news stories over the years and offer a few little clues about the Hotel Statler that used to be.

The world-famous Mr. and Mrs. Vernon Castle appeared at the Hippodrome in Cleveland often, and their celebrated dancing act featured the foxtrot. It was during Irvin Berlin's first Broadway show, *Watch Your Step*, in 1914 that the couple refined and popularized the foxtrot. Castle announced in an advertisement that he would accept private dancing pupils at his suite in the Hotel Statler at thirty dollars an hour—an extravagant amount of money for the average dancer. But to the Castles, time was money.[99]

The Cleveland Advertising Club dedicated its new home in the Statler on October 7, 1914. It was the largest club of its kind in the world with the finest quarters. William Ganson Rose was president and Thomas W. Garvin secretary.[100] The history of the Cleveland Advertising Club is legendary and merits its own tell-all book.

On May 12–14, 1914, the World Court Congress was held in Cleveland, proving one of the greatest inspirational gatherings in the city's history. Former president William Howard Taft, distinguished statesmen and national leaders representing many interests assembled to plan a world tribunal that would further universal peace. The most important public event was a luncheon given by the Cleveland Advertising Club on May 13 to the 250 nationally famous delegates in the ballroom of the Hotel Statler with more than 1,000 in attendance. At the speaker's table were John Hays Hammond, Mayor Newton D. Baker, Henry Clews, Judge Alton B. Parker, Rabbi Joseph Silverman, Professor Jeremiah W. Jenks, Dr. John Wesley Hill, Bainbridge Colby, W.W. Wilson, E.A. Filene, Judge D.D. Woodmansee, Samuel Mather, Theodore Marburg, Senator Atlee Pomerene, Emerson McMillin, George W. Kinney, James Brown Scott, Dr. Washington Gladden, Herbet S. Houston and William Ganson Rose, who presided. The enthusiasm of the meeting was remarkable; the audience rose more than twenty times to cheer the eloquence and patriotism of the eminent speakers. Unfortunately, this great step forward to peace was interrupted by World War I.[101]

BAD WEATHER ONE CANNOT SEE BUT FEEL

There is drama and excitement in really bad weather, in the driving snow and the lashing rain, the angry skies and the boiling lake. One of the most amazing persons in American history, Helen Keller, said it in her own way when she was trapped in her room at the Hotel Statler in Cleveland by the great blizzard that struck the city in early November 1913. It was one of the worst storms in Cleveland history. Twenty-one inches of snow were levied on the area by winds that reached a velocity of seventy-nine miles an hour, and life in the community came to a standstill for most of a week. Even without sight or hearing, as she was, Miss Keller's impressions of the storm, as related to a reporter for the *Cleveland Press*, were vivid:

> *I am stirred to the depth of my being by the storm and my body, mind and soul are better for this experience—the greatest of its kind in my life.*

Few times in my life has it been given me to feel sensations akin to those I have experienced as a captive of the blizzard in Cleveland during Sunday, Monday and Tuesday.

I knew it was storming before I was told. The rooms, the corridors, everywhere within the building, vibrated with the power of the storm without—when I knew it was snowing as it never had before in this part of the world, I wished to rush out and throw myself into the snow and ride upon the tempest. I raised my window, the gale blew upon me; as I was in the evening dress the wind stung my chest, but I loved it. I put my hands in the snow on the windowsill. It was softer than the softest down. I made a ball of it and pressed it to my cheek. I drank deep of its odor, for it has an odor soft and sweet as the daintiest perfume.[102]

The Stillman Theater

A longtime neighbor to the Hotel Statler was the Stillman Theater. The theater was a glorious partner for the hotel, and many of the Statler patrons found a precious escape inside the venue. The Stillman Theater was built on the site of the Stillman Hotel (see the preface), which was razed in 1902. The theater itself was not constructed until 1916, just before the new Statler was finished.[103] The Stillman was the first true movie palace in Cleveland, one of the largest and most luxurious ever built in the Sixth City. It had one screen and 1,800 seats—a very sizeable theater for its time.

Loews Theaters acquired the Stillman in the early 1920s and renamed it the Loews Stillman Theater. In 1939, the Stillman was the site of the Cleveland premiere of *Gone with the Wind*. During the 1950s, the Stillman had installed the Super Technirama 70 into its movie theater as a strategy to discourage the declining population of moviegoers from staying home and watching TV. By 1963, Loews management decided to close the wonderful theater. In 1965, most of the theater was demolished and replaced by a parking garage. However, even today, if one were to walk by the garage opening near East Twelfth Street and Euclid Avenue and peer inside, one would see the old columns of the theater built into the garage opening.

Final Thoughts on the Statler

The Hotel Statler, now the Statler Arms, still sits proudly on Euclid Avenue. It is a strong and memorable building. It still is the bosom buddy of the Union Club and once the Cleveland Athletic Club (now closed) across the street. The stately building has seen the prosperous city falter and now is a key part of Cleveland's downtown renaissance. Once a stately hotel, it now operates as an apartment complex and is nearly full of tenants. Still, the old Terrace Room, the ballroom and the lounge room sit empty. Additionally, the Swango's restaurant that operated during the 1970s and 1980s near the rear of the hotel on East Twelfth Street, too, sits empty. The building is close to being a dynamic place but needs to embrace the change all around it and redevelop the various empty spaces in its confines. The ghosts of the Hotel Statler whisper to us the amazing history of this most remarkable building. And we should listen.

The original Hotel Statler building before its expansion. *Photo courtesy of the Western Reserve Historical Society.*

A postcard showing the grand stature of the Hotel Statler on Euclid Avenue. *Photo courtesy of the Western Reserve Historical Society.*

Hotel workers strike against the Hotel Statler, drawing a big crowd. *Photo courtesy of the Cleveland Public Library.*

Left: The beautiful actress Olivia De Havilland talking to an admiring fan at the Hotel Statler. *Photo courtesy of the* Cleveland Press *Archives.*

Below: The Terrace Room at the Hotel Statler. *Photo courtesy of the* Cleveland Press *Archives.*

The private dining room at the Hotel Statler. *Photo courtesy of the* Cleveland Press *Archives.*

Euclid Avenue is busy near the front door of the Hotel Statler. *Photo courtesy of the* Cleveland Press *Archives.*

Left: Chef Clovis Chartron serves up an egg to Miss Elise Mulligan. *Photo courtesy of the* Cleveland Press *Archives.*

Below: The grand ballroom of the Hotel Statler. *Photo courtesy of the* Cleveland Press *Archives.*

NOTES

1. Philip W. Porter, *Cleveland: Confused City on a Seesaw* (Columbus: Ohio State University Press, 1976).
2. Ibid.
3. William Ganson Rose, *Cleveland: The Making of a City*, 2nd ed. (Kent, OH: Kent State University Press, 1990).
4. A. Parrish, "Alcazar Is a Spanish Castle in Cleveland Heights," *(Cleveland) Plain Dealer*, October 7, 1923, 19A.
5. A.E. Donkin, "The Alcazar Hotel: Cleveland Heights' First (and Only) 'Palace Hotel,'" *View from the Overlook* 28 (2011): 1–8.
6. Ibid.
7. E. Theiss, "Cleveland Heights' Alcazar Exudes Exotic Grace in Any Age," *(Cleveland) Plain Dealer*, October 12, 2008.
8. *(Cleveland) Plain Dealer*, "Allerton Club Residence."
9. K.L. Siemon, "Living in Tune," *(Cleveland) Plain Dealer*, January 7, 1985, 6-B.
10. Ganson Rose, *Cleveland.*
11. *(Cleveland) Plain Dealer*, "Allerton Club Residence."
12. Ganson Rose, *Cleveland.*
13. Ibid.
14. *(Cleveland) Plain Dealer*, "Failing Hotel Opened in '26 as Residence Club," May 28, 1971.
15. Archer H. Shaw, *The Plain Dealer: One Hundred Years in Cleveland* (New York: Alfred A. Knopf, 1942).
16. Ganson Rose, *Cleveland.*
17. George E. Condon, *Cleveland: The Best Kept Secret* (New York: Doubleday & Company, 1967).

18. Eric Johannesen, *Cleveland Architecture: 1876–1976*. (Cleveland, OH: Western Reserve Historical Society, 1979).
19. Ganson Rose, *Cleveland*.
20. Wikipedia, "Hotel Hollenden," November 10, 2013, http://en.wikipedia.org/wiki/Hollenden_Hotel (accessed January 16, 2014).
21. Shaw, *Plain Dealer*.
22. Robert I. Vexler, *Cleveland: A Chronological & Documentary History* (Dobbs Ferry, NY: Oceana Publications, 1977).
23. Shaw, *Plain Dealer*.
24. D.D. Van Tassel and J.J. Grabowski, *The Dictionary of Cleveland Biography* (Bloomington: Indiana University Press, 1996).
25. Heidi Fearing, "Weddell House/Rockefeller Building," Cleveland Historical, http://clevelandhistorical.org/items/show/247 (accessed April 13, 2014).
26. D. Simmons, "The Best Barber in America: George A. Myers," Teaching Cleveland, http://www.teachingcleveland.org/index.php?option=com_content&view=article&id=800:the-best-barber-in-america-george-a-myers&catid=150:african-american-history-in-cleveland&Itemid=173 (accessed April 14, 2014).
27. B. House-Soremekun, *Confronting the Odds: African-American Entrepreneurship in Cleveland, Ohio* (Kent, OH: Kent State University Press, 2002).
28. Ganson Rose, *Cleveland*.
29. Condon, *Cleveland*.
30. Ibid..
31. Ibid.
32. D. Tabler, "How Dino Crocetti of Steubenville Became Pop Singer Dean Martin," Appalachian History, April 9, 2013, http://www.appalacianhistory.net/2013/04/how-dino-of-steubenville-bacame-pop-singer-dean-martin.html (accessed January 28, 2014).
33. Ganson Rose, *Cleveland*.
34. Ibid.
35. Ibid.
36. *New York Times*, "H.L. Woodward Kills Himself in Cleveland," March 29, 1905, 2.
37. Ganson Rose, *Cleveland*.
38. Ibid.
39. Ibid.
40. Wikipedia, "Raymond T. Miller," December 12, 2012, http://en.wikipedia.org/wiki/Raymond_T._Miller (accessed March 2, 2014).
41. Condon, *Cleveland*.
42. Ibid.
43. Porter, *Cleveland*.
44. Ganson Rose, *Cleveland*.
45. Ibid.
46. Ibid.
47. Condon, *Cleveland*.
48. Van Tassel and Grabowski, *Dictionary of Cleveland Biography*.

49. R.D. Klyver, "North Union Shaker Community," Encyclopedia of Cleveland History, http://ech.case.edu/cgi/article.pl?id=NUSC (accessed April 14, 2014).
50. Van Tassel and Grabowski, *Dictionary of Cleveland Biography*.
51. Condon, *Cleveland*.
52. Johannesen, *Cleveland Architecture: 1876–1976*.
53. Ibid.
54. Wikipedia, "Terminal Tower," http://en.wikipedia.org/wiki/Terminal_Tower (accessed April 15, 2014).
55. Ganson Rose, *Cleveland*.
56. Condon, *Cleveland*.
57. Ganson Rose, *Cleveland*.
58. Ibid.
59. Ibid.
60. Eric Trickey, "Renaissance Cleveland Hotel," *Cleveland Magazine* (December 1, 2011).
61. Alea Lytle, "Kingsbury Run," *Cleveland Historical*, http://clevelandhistorical.org/items/show/376#.UvzXP3m9-fE (accessed February 13, 2014).
62. Trickey, "Renaissance Cleveland Hotel."
63. Marilyn Bardsley, "The Kingsbury Run Murders," *Crime Library*, http://www.crimelibrary.com/serial_killers/unsolved/kingsbury/8d.html (accessed February 13, 2014).
64. Lisa Alleman and F.X. O'Grady, "Hotel Cleveland," Cleveland Historical, http://clevelandhistorical.org/items/show/465#.U-DLxyiBXwx (accessed January 1, 2014).
65. J.G. Monnett Jr., "Name Hotel for Alexander Winton," *Cleveland Leader*, April 9, 1916.
66. Ibid.
67. W.S. McKinstry, "Alexander Winston: An Unsung Genius," *Historical Society News* 26, no. 8 (1972).
68. *The Book of Clevelanders* (Cleveland, OH: Burrows Brothers Company, 1914).
69. McKinstry, "Alexander Winston: An Unsung Genius."
70. "The Auto Aviation Museum Wing," *Historical Society News* 19, no. 9 (1965).
71. "Mr. Winton Makes a Sale," *Great Moments in the Ohio Heritage* 1, no. 8 (1961).
72. "Winton: The King of Cars," Second Chance Garage, http://www.secondchancegarage.com/public4/winton-the-king-of-cars-1.cfm (accessed January 15, 2014).
73. Richard E. Karberg and James A. Toman, *Euclid Avenue: Cleveland's Sophisticated Lady, 1920–1970*, 3rd ed. (Cleveland, OH: Cleveland Landmarks Press, 2002).
74. Wikipedia, "Artie Shaw," http://en.wikipedia.org/wiki/Artie_Shaw (accessed May 3, 2014).
75. J. Mosbrook, "Jazzed in Cleveland, Part 38," Cleveland: The New American City, June 22, 1998, http://www.cleveland.oh.us/wmv_news/jazz38.htm (accessed January 15, 2014).
76. *Milwaukee Journal*, "Hotel Blaze Claims 7 Lives in Cleveland," April 14, 1971.
77. Ganson Rose, *Cleveland*.

78. Ibid.
79. *(Lakewood) West County Advocate*, "The Lake Shore Hotel," February 8, 1930.
80. W. Salisbury, "An Art Deco Renaissance," *Plain Dealer Magazine*, November 13, 1988, 39–42.
81. *(Cleveland) Plain Dealer*, "Dance Under Glass at Lake Shore," October 27, 1929.
82. H. Allen, "Club 'Way Up in the Sky' Latest Addition to City's Night Life," *(Cleveland) Plain Dealer*, April 27, 1934.
83. *(Cleveland) Plain Dealer*, "Overall Robber Holds Up Hotel," October 7, 1929.
84. D. Chabek, "Lake Shore Towers Was Gold Coast's Mother Lode," *Lakewood Sun Post*, January 23, 1992, A8.
85. Ganson Rose, *Cleveland.*
86. Ibid.
87. Johannesen, *Cleveland Architecture: 1876–1976.*
88. Ganson Rose, *Cleveland.*
89. Wikipedia, "Hotel Statlers," December 31, 2013, http://en.wikipedia.org/wiki/Statler_Hotels (accessed January 1, 2014).
90. I. Sestanj, "Mafia at Cleveland's Hotel Statler," An Intrepid Traveler's Blog, May 31, 2011, http://shekoos.wordpress.com (accessed January 20, 2014).
91. "Novel Ideas in Managing City's Largest Hotel," *New York Times Magazine*, June 3, 1917.
92. M. Byrnes, "The Rise and Fall of One of America's Most Innovative Hotel Chains," Atlantic Cities, February 15, 2013, http://www.theatlanticcities.com (accessed January 20, 2014).
93. W. French, "Statler Bar Opens 'Frenzied' Season," *Cleveland Press*, November 9, 1937.
94. *(Cleveland) Plain Dealer*, "Statler Terrace in Debut for 400," November 9, 1937.
95. Ibid.
96. James M. Wood, *Out & About with Winsor French* (Kent, OH: Kent State University Press, 2011).
97. T. Schwarz, *Shocking Stories of the Cleveland Mob*, 2nd ed. (Charleston, SC: The History Press, 2010).
98. Ibid.
99. Ganson Rose, *Cleveland.*
100. Ibid.
101. Ibid.
102. Condon, *Cleveland.*
103. B. Krefft, "Loews Stillman Theater," Cinema Treasures, http://cinematreasures.org/theaters/3731 (accessed January 20, 2014).

INDEX

ABOUT THE AUTHOR

Michael has enjoyed working with and for some of the best companies in the northeast Ohio area. Although not a native Clevelander, Michael is known for his unshakeable belief in a great future for Cleveland and Cleveland-based businesses. The best things in his life—both personally and professionally—have happened in Cleveland. Michael is perhaps best known for his term with the City of Cleveland as the senior executive for technology development, or "tech czar," where he was responsible for the economic development of the technology industries in the city. During his tenure as the "tech czar," Michael was able to recruit thirty-seven tech companies into the city of Cleveland, which created many much-needed jobs for the city and revenue for other city businesses.

He is currently the tech columnist for the *Plain Dealer* and co-host of Cleveland Confidential Radio. Michael was recently the regional vice-president for the Cleveland operations of Expedient, a Pittsburgh, Pennsylvania–based data collocation and managed services company. Michael was also the co-founder and chief financial officer of BlueBridge Networks, a Cleveland-based provider of data center services. Michael also co-founded and is a major investor in EmergingChefs.com, a Cleveland-based culinary event and content company. He also worked for LNE Group, FIT Technologies, Saltz, Shamis & Goldfarb, Ernst & Young and National City Venture Capital.

Michael has spoken at numerous national economic development, technology and social media events, including NOTACON, Gov 2.5, the Online Marketing Summit and the Cool Twitter Conference. He appeared on the Fox News channel's *John Stoessel Show* and was included in the Drew Carey–supported Reason Foundation documentary titled *Reason Saves Cleveland*.

Michael earned his MBA from Case Western Reserve University and his bachelor's degree from Xavier University. He is the author of *Lost Cleveland*, a short history of some of the leading architectural wonders of Cleveland, which was published by The History Press in late 2010. He currently lives in Lakewood, Ohio, with his fiancée, Nora, and their young daughter, Ileana.